CD 5u

MANSFIELD

The Story of Vermont's Loftiest Mountain

By Robert L. Hagerman

Library of Congress Catalog Card Number 70-181081

FIRST EDITION

PRINTED IN THE UNITED STATES OF AMERICA
BY
ESSEX PUBLISHING COMPANY, INC.
ESSEX JUNCTION, VERMONT

COVER PHOTOGRAPHS: **Front** — In this view of Mt. Mansfield, photographed by the Author, it was a time of changing seasons with the spring green of the Stowe valley contrasting with winter snow remaining on the mountain; house and barn in the foreground are part of the Sugar House Hill development on Vermont 108. **Back** — The great cleft of Smuggler's Notch as seen from the Mt. Mansfield Toll Road; this photograph is also by the Author.

CONTENTS

Map Of
Mt. Mansfield Region

Trails And Features Identified

TRAILS

1. Lake Mansfield
2. Nebraska Notch
3. Butler Lodge
4. Maple Ridge
5. Haselton
6. Halfway House
7. Sunset Ridge
8. Laura Cowles
9. Forehead Long Trail
10. Taft Lodge Long Trail
11. Hell Brook
12. Bear Pond
13. Wallace Cutoff
14. Wampahoofus
15. Forehead Bypass
16. Rock Garden
17. Frost
18. Cliff
19. Monument
20. Profanity
21. Story
22. Cantilever Rock
23. Adam's Apple
24. Hell Brook Cutoff
25. Amherst
26. Elephant's Head
27. Back Nose
28. Triangle
29. South Link
30. Lakeview
31. Canyon
32. Canyon North
33. Canyon North Extension
34. The Subway

OTHER FEATURES

A. Hambone's Crater
B. Rock of Terror and Balance Rock
C. Drift Rocks
D. Grant Monument (Frenchman's Pile)
E. March of Dimes Monument
F. Wampahoofus Rock

CAUTIONARY NOTE: The reader should *not* use this map by itself as a trails guide to the Mt. Mansfield Region. He is strongly urged to obtain copies of the Green Mountain Club's official Mansfield Region Trail Map and its *Guide Book of The Long Trail* which provide important information on the different trails including detailed descriptions and ratings of difficulty. Visitors to the mountain should also note that Vermont Forests and Parks Department regulations ban camping and campfires in the Mt. Mansfield State Forest except in designated areas, and prohibit littering and the picking of protected plant life (detailed regulations are posted in several places on the mountain). The University of Vermont has similar regulations for the summit ridge property which it owns.

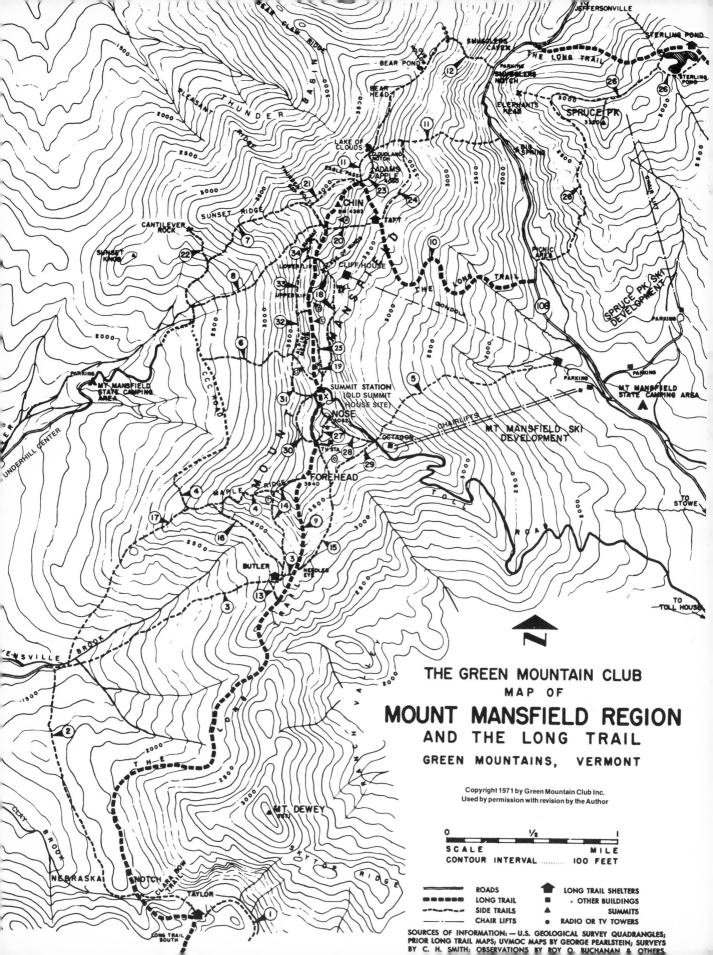

THE GREEN MOUNTAIN CLUB
MAP OF
MOUNT MANSFIELD REGION
AND THE LONG TRAIL
GREEN MOUNTAINS, VERMONT

Copyright 1971 by Green Mountain Club Inc.
Used by permission with revision by the Author

0   1/8   1
SCALE   MILE
CONTOUR INTERVAL .... 100 FEET

▬▬▬▬ ROADS	🛖 LONG TRAIL SHELTERS
▬ ▬ ▬ LONG TRAIL	■ OTHER BUILDINGS
- - - SIDE TRAILS	▲ SUMMITS
—·—·— CHAIR LIFTS	● RADIO OR TV TOWERS

SOURCES OF INFORMATION: — U.S. GEOLOGICAL SURVEY QUADRANGLES;
PRIOR LONG TRAIL MAPS; UVMOC MAPS BY GEORGE PEARLSTEIN; SURVEYS
BY C. H. SMITH; OBSERVATIONS BY ROY O. BUCHANAN & OTHERS.

CHAPTER
1

Legends, Lore and Literature

OUR STORY BEGINS IN 1609 with a Frenchman and his large party of Indian *voyageurs* as they paddled canoes down the huge lake between what became Vermont and New York. The Frenchman was Samuel de Champlain, after whom the lake was named, and he was the first white man to view Mt. Mansfield. It was to be another 154 years before the mountain received that name and seven more before another white man became the first to set foot on its bulk.

Since then this loftiest of Vermont's Green Mountains has become a key thread in the fabric of local heritage, particularly that of the towns of Stowe, Cambridge and Underhill, among which the mountain is divided. The use of the mountain's name is one facet of this.

In Stowe there is the Mt. Mansfield Company, Inc., operator of one of the state's major ski areas. There is also the long-established Mt. Mansfield Garage and the trolley line which once ran between Stowe and Waterbury was the Mt. Mansfield Electric Railroad. The town once had the Mt. Mansfield Maple Merchants, the Mt. Mansfield Creamery and a Mansfield Mt. Grange.

In the town of Cambridge is the Mansfield Chapter of the Order of Eastern Star, the Mount Mansfield Post of the American Legion and, in the past, a Mansfield Lodge of the International Order of Odd Fellows. And in Underhill is the Mansfield Woman's Club and at one time the Mt. Mansfield Civic Club. This town shares with others in support of the Mt. Mansfield Union High School in neighboring Jericho. There is even a ferryboat named Mt. Mansfield which plies the waters of Lake Champlain.

In Stowe the Mansfield Dairy has a long-established trademark which provides an especially colorful note on our mountain's place in the town. This is a picture carried on the dairy's delivery trucks and milk containers of a cow on skis, scarf flying as she comes down the mountain and proclaiming, "Mt. Mansfield, Stowe, Vt. *Thrills Me.*"

The figure was conceived by Mrs. Dorothy Nelson in 1939 when she and her husband, Clyde, acquired the business. "The idea came from the old Borden cow, Elsie," Mrs. Nelson told the writer. "I drew it up and sent it off to a company in New York State somewhere which applied it to our bottles. They revised the figure somewhat and added the scarf. Their cow was better than mine but my mountain was better." The Nelsons also had the figure added to their delivery truck and from that beginning a local tradition was born.

In 1943 Carroll Pike acquired the business and faithfully continued the trademark on both trucks and containers. He noted with regret the changeover he eventually had to make from round, high-necked bottles to square ones; "The cow doesn't show up as pretty on those," he told the writer. The figure is also now used on the dairy's paper cartons as well. In late 1970 Pike leased the business to Winford Small who will continue to use the unique promotional figure for Mt. Mansfield skiing.

In the dairy state that is Vermont our mountain appropriately enough has figured in the naming of cows as well. At least a few were those of the late Dorman N. Safford whose Mansfield Farm was located in Cambridge. In the early 1900's he had a number of registered Holstein-Friesian cattle in his herd including *Mansfield Dorfland Queen* and *Mansfield Clothilde 2d.*

A special note of interest regarding the mountain involves the U.S. Mails. The week of May 15, 1938 was National Air Mail Week and for the occasion the Stowe Rotary Club sponsored a special envelope cachet for air mail letters leaving the local post office. The imprint showed Mt. Mansfield's profile with skiers descending together with the caption, "Skiing At Its Best." Commercial artwork involving the mountain includes a handsome etching of Mansfield inaugurated in 1953 by the Lamoille County Bank of Hyde Park on patrons' checks and its own letterhead stationery.

And in Underhill Center the Saint Thomas Catholic Church describes itself as "under Mansfield's mantle," a phrase coined by its current pastor, the Rev. Bernard F. Depeaux, not long after his arrival the summer of 1966. Father Depeaux subsequently organized a church-community Dixieland jazz band known as the *Mt. Mansfield Mantleers* in a further adaptation of the now quite well-established church tradition.

Much has been made of the famous Mansfield ridgeline which nature left in a profile of a man's face complete with Forehead, Nose, Upper and Lower Lips, Chin and even Adam's Apple. A number of legends also exist to account for the mountain's formation and present-day appearance.

One is the tale of Mishawaka the Indian which was put in written form in the early 1920's by Roxanna Thomas (French), then of Cambridge. The story begins in the time when Indians lived in the valley at Mansfield's base. The mountain then was not shaped as it is to-day but was simply a great mound of rock without a distinguishing feature. At the very top the Indians had built an altar where they worshipped the rising sun. The trail to this was so steep and treacherous that only the strongest braves could endure the climb.

Mishawaka was the son of the tribe's chief, a noble young brave except that he was severely crippled as a result of an accident. It was torture for him to walk even a few steps and for that reason he had never climbed the mountain to carry out the traditional worship.

In the course of time Mishawaka's father died and custom dictated that he should become the new chief. But others of the tribe objected to having as their leader a lame weakling who had never been able to climb the mountain to worship. Word of this disaffection reached Mishawaka and he immediately resolved to correct the situation by climbing to the summit altar even if it meant dying in the effort. He left the Indian village unnoticed and for days crawled and pulled himself along despite the agonizing pain. Finally, exhausted and terribly weak, he reached the top of the mountain just as the sun was rising. Miss Thomas provided the finale in these words.

> "The impossible is achieved. I have reached the summit altar and I am fully repaid by the sight," murmured Mishawaka, and slipped to the ground dead.

> For days a terrible storm raged about the mountain and the summit was hidden by a dense bank of clouds.

> The Indians in the village were frightened by the fury of the storm. But behold when the tempest was over and the clouds were lifted from the mountain the Indians gazed in wonder at the shape of Mount Mansfield. No longer was it simply a

pile of rocks, but its outline was that of a human face. And that face was the image of Mishawaka's....

Another legend takes the form of a long poem composed by William E. Marrs back in 1867. It deals with a conflict between two mythical female figures: Nephele, "a nymph too fair for mortal kind" who in earlier days dwelled at the base of the mountain, and Frigia, the "ice-crowned Queen" whose realm was the top of Mansfield, then completely frozen over. A handsome fisherman appears on the scene and settles in with Nephele. But he is drawn irresistibly to climb to the icy summit where "He entered cold Frigia's portals/ And passed from the knowledge of men!"

Nephele is a woman scorned. She rouses her elements of thunder and lightning, wind, hail and rain and directs them to avenge her by putting Frigia to flight so that Nephele herself can assume the loftier realm. Three days of tempest ensue

> But when at last the war cloud rolled away
> And once again the frightened face of day
> Looked down in wonder on the fearful scene,
> Behold, the snow bound hills were robed in green!

And so Mansfield became a proper Green Mountain and perhaps Nephele may still be found there.

A third legend of Mansfield's formation originally appeared in a little newspaper in Stowe which was published just one time on August 17, 1858. This has to do with a giant from "the far off South" who many years ago was walking northward on an exploratory journey when he arrived in the Stowe area. At this point "... being fatigued with his journey, as night came on he laid him down to sleep, and unfortunately ... he has never since awoke, but like a giant Rip Van Winkle sleeps on, and will for aught we know for infinite ages to come."

The final legend turned up by this writer is another poem, this one entitled "The Talk of the Mountains" and written by Rev. Perrin B. Fisk in 1890. This tale of Mansfield's formation has a close association with Camel's Hump, a sister mountain a short distance to the south. The lengthy poem contains several elements but of interest here is the following:

> The "Camel's Hump" is there on high; his head, as you might think,
> Is by the river's bed where once he ran to kneel and drink,
> But, stumbling in his thirsty haste, he threw his rider high,
> And there lies "Mansfield" as he fell, a-staring at the sky:
> This dashing youth, a giant in his pride, (say naught of birth,)
> Had laid a bet on time to ride the "Camel" round the earth,
> But—weary, being over-driven—here ended all his pacing;
> And th' Fates condemned them there to lie, as a warning against *racing*.

With that cautionary note on the hazards of high-speed camel-riding we shall leave the legends of Mansfield and turn to another form of folklore associated with the mountain — weather predicting. One of the more well-established beliefs is that winter will arrive in force six weeks after the first fall of snow that is sufficient to whiten the mountain. One Cambridge native, John Safford, told the writer he has found this Mansfield weather indicator to be "quite close and regular."

Some other Mansfield weather signals were passed on to the writer by two Underhill Center residents, Albert Steinhour and his sister, Mrs. Jesse Luck. In the summertime, they say, when the mountain looks "wavy" a big storm or heavy wind is on its way. When the mountain looks black a cold wave is coming. And when a cold spell has frosted the mountain white and it then takes on a blue appearance that means warmer weather will soon arrive.

In the field of literature a number of poems have been written specifically about Mt. Mansfield. Not surprisingly, each author generally glorifies the mountain's natural setting and often adds philosophical or religious nuances. An undated poem by Oella A. Thompson follows:

MT. MANSFIELD

Serene, rugged old mountain
With face upturned toward the sky,
Heedless of the roar of the tempest,
Which leaps down your sides with a cry;
But always in calm meditation,
Your face toward the infinite raised.
Grandly sublime, you seem waiting
Till Creation joins in pean of praise.

Again, when the clouds form a pillow,
The face seems so gently to rest,
With almost a smile on the features
By the billowy softness caressed.
Then Mansfield, majestic, looks human,
The face raised to heaven above
As if 'twas not alone man, but mountain,
Should share in God's care and his love.

Mt. Mansfield also has a place in other forms of artistic endeavor. One of the more unusual is a Tiffany stained-glass window at the Proctor Union Church in Proctor, just north of Rutland; this was created in the special and highly renowned process developed by The Louis E. Tiffany Studios of New York City. The window is one of a series of three along one wall which depict different Vermont scenes with each in a different season of the year (a fourth window for the fourth season, not a Tiffany, was added at a later time). *The First Window*, as it is identified, represents Spring and portrays Mt. Mansfield and the Underhill valley as viewed from Westford. This was the childhood home of Mrs. Minnie E. Proctor in whose memory the window was presented to the church by her children. Mrs. Proctor was the wife of Fletcher D. Proctor, governor of Vermont from 1906 to 1908 and a member of the family long associated with the state's marble industry as well as its political life.

But it is with sketching pencil, watercolor and oil paint that our mountain has been committed countless times to paper and canvas, by amateurs and professionals alike. Note of only two special renderings, both in oils, can be made here though there are undoubtedly others. One was a painting of the mountain by R.W. Hubbard accepted for exhibition at the Paris Exposition of 1867. The other was a painting of Mansfield by Edward Martin Taber which was purchased by the Metropolitan Museum of Art in New York City in 1926.

Taber holds a special place in Stowe's history. An accomplished artist, he lived at his family's fine home known as Four Winds Farm on Taber Hill for several years before a premature death in 1896. He established a close attachment to the Stowe area and, as a writer of some note as well, committed many of his observations of rural life and natural phenomena to a journal which, together with other of his writings, was subsequently published.

On a number of occasions Taber writes specifically of Mt. Mansfield, describing its changing appearance at different seasons and under different weather conditions. One example: "The Mountain is seen at its best in winter, with snow and ice along the rocky summit. . . . In this hoary coating it seems like some great Colossus, maimed and time-eaten, more majestic, more inscrutable, with loftier riddles than the Sphinx."

At another point Taber provides testimony to the old saying that absence makes the heart grow fonder. He was riding a train along the west side of Lake Champlain and in looking out the window and across the lake:

> . . . with a sudden emotion I recognized that mighty form. Though dwarfed and disproportioned, there lay the great profile, the chin heaved up against the sky, and all the lesser Green Mountains clustered around it . . . calm and reposeful, the sleeping giant with his awful and passionless countenance.

> My Mountain! With a swelling heart, with the rise of emotion that shakes the voice and brings tears to the eyes, I looked back at Mount Mansfield. Clouds, touched by the setting sun, rested upon the highest point of the chin, and above them, white as smoke, hung the moon. The sight was borne in upon me like the swelling strains of some immortal music. . . .

As Mt. Mansfield bulks large physically in its local setting so it has figuratively bulked large in the mind and heart of individuals and in the lives of the communities which surround it. Moving closer to this noble mountain let's begin by learning how it came to have the name that it does.

CHAPTER 2

Mansfield, The Name

HOW DID THIS PLACE get its name?" is an easy enough question to ask but, like many another query, often difficult to answer. Mansfield, an appropriately solid Anglo-Saxon name for this capstone of Vermont, bears a full share of disagreement as to its origin though it perhaps is not quite so colorful as some other place names in the state.

Appropriate to our case here was the naming of Camel's Hump mountain which lies about 15 miles to the south of Mansfield. Ira Allen, of whom we will shortly hear more, referred to it on a map in 1798 as "The Camel's Rump." Zadock Thompson used this name in 1824 in his first gazetteer of the state. But in later books he changed it to Camel's Hump, the name now officially accepted and in common use.* More heated controversy has raged over "Le Lion Couchant," the name said to have been given this dramatic peak by Samuel de Champlain. Some have translated this as the "Crouching Lion" to the dismay of devotees who insist that it should be the "Couching Lion," signifying rest and repose rather than alertness or imminence of attack.

The first name for *our* mountain was Moze-o-de-be-Wadso meaning Mountain-With-A-Head-Like-A-Moose. It was christened this by the Abnaki Indians, a tribe of the great Algonquin family which once ranged through this area.

As to the name Mansfield, several theories about its origin have been offered over the years. These are: an etymological approach in which Mansfield is said to derive from the couplet of words, Man's Field; a physiographic approach somewhat related to the first in the resemblance of the mountain's ridgeline to a man's profile; in a more pedestrian approach, the derivation of the name from another place of the same name; and finally, an honorific approach in which a prominent English jurist figures. Related to all of these is the fact that our mountain is situated in what originally was the town of Mansfield.

Reference to the first theory is made by "R.L.P." of Stowe in a letter to a Montpelier newspaper in 1861; he states that "Considered etymologically, the name *Mansfield, man's field*, may seem somewhat inappropriate for a locality so little adapted to agricultural purposes, as [is] this grand, picturesque and sublime repose..."

Maria N. Wilkins in her 1871 history of Stowe appears to give short shrift to the "man's field" theory, at least when it came to an *in situ* inspection, and also touches on the

*Thompson apparently was embarrassed about the first name right from the start. In that 1824 gazetteer he added a footnote to his description of Camel's Rump in the form of a question, "Why not Camel's Hump?"

second theory. She takes note of the "fancied or real resemblance of these Mountains to the face of a man lying on his back" but then says that "The writer is of the opinion that an examination of its face *on* the mountain would never have suggested the name of *Mansfield.*"

Both the third and fourth theories presume that the mountain did indeed take its name from the town of Mansfield so that the question then becomes where the town got its name. It was on June 8, 1763 — a year which is critical to the resolution of this question — that Governor Benning Wentworth of the King of England's New Hampshire Province issued a charter for what was identified as the Town of Mansfield to 64 grantees or original proprietors. Clearly the name for the town dates from this time. The question thus becomes why was this name used and who applied it to the new township.

In an article on Mt. Mansfield for the magazine *Appalachia*, Llew Evans in 1944 wrote:

> Old Wentworth, planning his historic landgrab, probably just cross-hatched a crude map of the country into townships six miles square and labeled them with whatever English place names came to his mind: Stowe, Middlesex, Bolton, Sterling, Mansfield. Mt. Mansfield, like Sterling Mountain, merely took its name from the township someone found it in.

Other writers have made a direct connection between Mansfield in England and the Vermont township while still others have related the name to the earlier settled towns of Mansfield, Mass. and Mansfield, Conn. The latter theories were both laid to rest by Dr. W.G.E. Flanders, proprietor of an inn on Mansfield's west flank during the 1920's and early 1930's.

Their flaw, according to the doctor, lies in the chronology of events. In a report on his conclusions, it is noted that some of the original proprietors of the new Wentworth grant were from Norton, Mass., a portion of which town later was called Mansfield after the English Chief Justice, Lord Mansfield. The presumption is that these men applied the name of that town to the block of their new holdings. But, the report states, "It appears ... that Mansfield, Massachusetts, was not known as such until April 26, 1770, when a portion of the Town of Norton was set apart under that name. This was seven years after the Hampshire grant of Mansfield." Similarly, the article continues, "Another theory is that Mansfield, Vermont, was named after Mansfield, Conn. But Mansfield, Conn., was set off from Windham, Conn., in 1774, or 11 years after the Hampshire grant of the land which became Mansfield, Vermont."

Thus, concluded Dr. Flanders, who was reported to have given "considerable study" to the matter, "it is safe to assume the land ... later called Mansfield, Vermont, was the first grant or town to be named after Lord Mansfield of England." Other writers, including Evans, also referred to the Lord Mansfield theory but dispatched it on the basis that William Murray, the English jurist in question, did not receive his elevation to a peerage title until several years *after* the charter for the Mansfield grant had been issued. But they were in error here.

Who was this William Murray, 1st Earl of Mansfield? According to the Encyclopedia Britannica, he was born in 1705 in Scotland where he subsequently established himself as a lawyer. But he did not have much experience or much of a name in English legal circles until 1737 when a "a single speech in one jury trial placed him at the head of the bar." In 1742 he was appointed solicitor general to the King and in 1754 was named attorney general.

In 1756 a vacancy occurred on the King's bench. Murray claimed the chief justiceship and at this time was made Baron Mansfield. Subsequently, in 1776, he was created Earl of Mansfield. The proper form of address for both of these titled positions is "Lord" so that Murray was indeed Lord Mansfield well before 1763 when the Hampshire grant of Mansfield was made. Thus it is certainly possible, from the standpoint of timing, that Lord Mansfield was the namesake for what became the Vermont township.

Murray continued as England's chief justice for 32 years until 1788 when he retired from the post. He died in 1793. His permanent stamp on Anglo-American jurisprudence lay in the field of commercial law where his decisions and other actions are said to have led to much reform in this area.

But of special significance to Vermont was Lord Mansfield's role in an important decision relating to the New Hampshire grants. What is now Vermont, which lies between the Connecticut River on the east and Lake Champlain on the west, was for a number of years in the 1700's an area of considerable dispute between the provinces of New York and New Hampshire. In 1752 Murray together with another crown official ruled that this area in question "is become a part of New Hampshire." Other evidence also gave weight to the New Hampshire province's claim to the disputed territory. But because of this particular decision, both Governor Benning Wentworth, who issued the Mansfield charter, and the original proprietors who received it certainly had good reason to honor Lord Mansfield by naming the new town after him. But which of the two did so is still uncertain and probably always will be.

In any event, after indicating that our mountain took its name from the town, Dr. Flanders concluded that "Mount Mansfield got its name from Lord Mansfield of England, in spite of some claims to the contrary." And so, in this way, our mountain emerged from anonymity with a halo of English glory.

The record, however, is not quite complete without a footnote to the effect that for much of the 19th century at least, the mountain was referred to as Mansfield Mountain or even Mansfield Mountains, the latter a reference to its several "peaks," that is, the Forehead, Nose and Chin. Later it became Mount Mansfield and today the name generally appears in its most abbreviated form, Mt. Mansfield.

CHAPTER
3

Mansfield, The Town

MANSFIELD, the town that is no more, may indeed have been but a cross-hatching on a map not only for Governor Benning Wentworth but also for those 64 original proprietors to whom Wentworth issued his charter. As far as is known, none of these men ever saw their wilderness acreage, much less settled there. They did, however, take steps to stake their claim, so to speak, and to refine that six-mile-square of 23,040 acres into a series of smaller lots within the original rights of about 327 acres each. And the man they engaged in 1772 to do this job of surveying was no less than Ira Allen, who subsequently played a leading role in the establishment of Vermont, first as an independent Republic in 1777 and then as the fourteenth of these United States to which Union it was admitted in 1791.

In an autobiography of his early years Allen recorded in some detail his connection with the town of Mansfield, a good chunk of which he owned for a short period of time. In carrying out the survey he may have been the first white man to climb to the summit of Mt. Mansfield and, if that was not done, certainly he and other members of his party ranged widely over the mountain's flanks and climbed at least once over the summit ridge if not the summit itself.

To carry out the survey contract for which he was to be paid 90 pounds Allen takes Capt. Remember Baker of Arlington into partnership with him and Baker carries major responsibility for preparing for the trip including the hiring of five other men. Allen first takes care of some other matters including the raising of cash and credit from a brother, Heman,* and then rejoins Baker and the others at an agreed-upon meeting place. After various difficulties including a near-violent encounter with another party of men, the group reaches Mansfield. They first set out the southwest corner of the town, Allen reports, and then while the other men established a camp there,

> . . . Capt. Baker with me set out to explore the town, which we found to consist of a tremendous range of Mountains, covered with evergreens near the centre of the town. [They climbed a tree on a high pinnacle and from there] could see over the town and a great country. At this time, I was owner of very near one third of the town, and could not discover lands that would [make] one good farm. This gave Baker an

*Another of Ira's brothers was Ethan Allen, leader of Vermont's Green Mountain Boys of Revolutionary War fame.

opportunity to pass many hard jokes on me respecting my purchase, &c.

While good farm land today certainly has value, Allen's observation makes it clear that land suitable for agriculture was of prime consideration at that time.

The two men proceeded to survey the town's outside boundaries and then the original rights and smaller 50-acre lots. The job was nearly complete when Baker cracked the glass on his compass so that Allen had to finish it himself. Late that same year Allen prepared a map from the survey. He then wanted not only to get paid those 90 pounds for the work but also to sell the rights that he owned in the town. But it seems, he reports, that "a difficulty arose in my mind," his solution for which might be called either shrewdness or downright dishonesty. To understand his report on this it helps to know that softwood trees, particularly the spruce and (balsam) fir which Allen mentions, are about the only kinds of trees which grow in the upper elevations of the Green Mountains. A report of their existence thus indicates mountainous terrain to a suitably knowledgable person. Records Allen of his "difficulty:"

> A great proportion of the corners of said lots were made on spruce or fir timber, and if I described them as such, it would show the poorness of the town, and raise many questions that I wished to avoid. I made use of a stratagem that answered my purpose. In my survey bills, I called spruce and fir gum-wood, a name not known by the people of Sharon (the place where the proprietors lived). They asked what kind of timber gumwood was. I told them tall Straight trees that had a gum, much like the gum on cherry trees &c.

While Allen does not explicitly say so, it is clear the proprietors accepted his explanation and, though this is hard to believe, apparently did not question him directly about the nature of the terrain he had found in their township. In any event a key part of Allen's anticipated difficulty had been adroitly side-stepped; the next was to sell his Mansfield rights and get his money for the survey. What follows suggests that Allen was the original Vermont horse-trader.

> While the proprietors were busy inspecting the map, Survey Bills, &c., I took aside the brother of one of the principal proprietors, who was an ignorant fellow and owned two rights in the town. I tried to buy his rights, but he dared not sell them without first consulting his brother. By this the proprietors all got the alarm that I wished to purchase, and land in Mansfield was considered of consequence. I was urged to sell back to the proprietors the twenty rights I had bought, which I did, and obtained the ninety pounds for the survey, &c., which I considered of more consequence than the whole town. Having closed this business satisfactorily to myself, I returned to my brother's and had a hearty laugh with my brothers Heman and Zimri, on informing them respecting the gum-wood &c.

Allen's account is apparently the only record relating to the earliest years of the Mansfield township and, by his terms, it is hardly a flattering one. The original and subsequent proprietors did meet and organize themselves in some fashion but few records of these early proceedings remain.

The honor of being the town's first settler is given to Zimri Luce (pronounced Zimeri with a long final "i") who arrived from Hartland, Vermont in 1799. One of his ten children, also named Zimri, nearly 75 years later recorded something of what his father and the family experienced. He first briefly reports on his own birth in 1795 in Hartland and on the elder Zimri's arrival in Mansfield. He then goes on in semi-literate but perfectly understandable style:

> [Father's] was the first family in town. I was about five years old ... Father came up and bought the land and gave $2 per acre — he went to Mr. Kaisers in Morristown and bought some grain for his family to live on when they come — when we moved father went to Mr Kaisers after his grain Mr Kaiser had sold it We had meal enough to last til first of May. Father had no money to buy grain so he started for Hartland on foot — The two or three weeks while he was gone we had nothing to eat but leeks [wild onions] they were very plenty on the meadow — we dug them and roasted or boild them, put butter on them as long as the butter lasted I remember I sufferd by hunger — When Father came home he brot meal enough to last us til August — He had a yoke of oxen at Hartland he got a crotched stick and drawd his meal to Stowe on that .. The Proprietors of Mansfield offerd a premium of one hundred acres of land to the first settlers — when the proprietors met a[t] Windsor, Father went to see them — They told him he must get his land out of each proprietors land — he said there were so many proprietors he would do nothing about it....

So it seems that in addition to all his other troubles the senior Zimri was effectively hoodwinked out of collecting the premium of land due him for settling in Mansfield.

Following close on Zimri's heels to the town were Samuel Henderson and Isaac Knight who are also said to have arrived in 1799. Another early settler was Moses Luce, a brother of the first Zimri's, though we don't have the date of his arrival. Another man early on the scene was a third Luce, Ivory, who was a nephew of the other two Mansfield Luces. He was a member of this family who was most closely connected with the development of the town and, as we shall shortly see, with a major fight against its eventual dissolution and annexation to other towns. Ivory arrived in the area in 1806 or 1807 — accounts vary.

A somewhat later settler was Lewis Harlow who came from Woodstock and made his "pitch" in Mansfield on what has since been known as Harlow Hill. Apparently Harlow wanted to leave his old home town with a clean slate for he inserted the following poetic notice, dated January 12, 1822, in the Woodstock newspaper.

> They said to me the other day
>   You sold your farm to move away.
> And if our books are just and true
>   A little something is our due.
> This is to let the people know
>   To Mansfield I intend to go:
> The first of March next
>   Is the time I have fixed.
> All those I have the luck to owe
>   Please to call and tell me so;
> Some I'll secure, the rest I'll pay;
>   It is not my intent to run away.

As Ira Allen made clear, there wasn't much arable land in Mansfield. It was only on the east side of our mountain that some clearing of woods for farming purposes took place. This division of the town by terrain helps to understand its later break-up and annexation to neighboring towns.

It wasn't until 1815 that sufficient settlers had arrived to organize the town. This occurred at a meeting on March 30 of that year when the first officers were elected and other steps taken to set up a town government under the then prevailing state laws. Records of this and later meetings of the town's voters are preserved at the Stowe Town Clerk's office. Based on his review of these records and probably other accounts, Stowe historian Walter J. Bigelow says that "residents [of Mansfield] were often in rivalry over the conduct of town business. The result was very turbulent meetings in which intimidation was attempted on a scale that would have landed the aggressors in state prison under the present election statutes." Who "aggressed" whom is not reported.

Town meeting troubles did not, however, retard the town's population growth. Census records show that in 1800 there were 12 inhabitants (all Zimri Luce's tribe), in 1810, 38, and in 1820, 60. By 1830 the number had increased sharply to 279, which is as many or more residents than a number of Vermont towns have today. But that was the high-water mark for by 1840 the official count had declined to 223.

It was in 1830 that agitation to have the town of Mansfield annexed to some other town or towns began. At a special meeting in May of that year voters registered their willingness to have the town divided, with the part "west of the top of the mountain" to be "set to Underhill" and the balance to Stowe. Apparently nothing happened for in 1834 another vote was recorded, this time for the annexation of the whole town to Stowe.

In 1839 the state Legislature did pass an act annexing the western part of the town to Underhill. Apparently no Mansfield residents opposed this loss but it was a different story when it came to the annexation of the remainder of the town to Stowe. (Here it might be noted that portions of Stowe which originally lay in Mansfield are the Luce and Harlow Hills already mentioned, the upper Nebraska Valley, the Ranch Camp area and part of Edson Hill.)

The matter lay dormant for several years but in 1847, by a count of 22 to 9, Mansfield voters once more said they wanted to be added to Stowe. In 1848 the Legislature responded with an act providing for the desired annexation. This, however, was subject to the final approval of the voters of both towns. On Dec. 9, 1848 Stowe voters accepted the annexation by a count of 176-81. Four days earlier, Mansfield voters had approved the merger by a similar solid majority, 34-18. Here the tale of Mansfield, the town, might have ended but for Ivory Luce. He proceeded on a campaign to preserve the township that leaves a variety of footnotes to its history. But first an introduction of the man.

Ivory carries the reputation of being "a hard man" and some of the things he is said to have done give reason for the characterization. One revealing story is told by a great-granddaughter, Mrs. Inez (Smith) Burnham, who was born and brought up on one of the Luce family farms. Ivory, she says, as a young man was living in Hartland like many of his relatives. One day he made an agreement with his father, also named Ivory, to cut up a large pile of wood. The elder Ivory for his part promised to give his son a new pair of boots which he was making. The latter proceeded to cut up all the wood but when he went to collect his due he learned that his father had sold the boots to another man. Young Ivory, according to Mrs. Burnham, "was so mad that he left town then and there and never went back."

But while Ivory may have been hard, she continued, he also felt concern for his fellow man. By way of illustration she reports that a sheriff had appeared at the house of a neighboring woman, who was a widow, to take a stove as payment for a debt which she had. "Ivory got word of the difficulty and promptly went to pay off the debt so the woman could keep her stove," Mrs. Burnham said.

So this was the man who hated to see the disappearance of his town. While he had not been the town's representative in that crucial 1848 session he had been elected to the post in a number of previous years, 1818-26, 1829, 1830, 1835, 1838 and 1847. As his first move he got the support of a sufficient number of Mansfield voters to get himself "elected" as town representative in 1849, by which time, of course, the Mansfield township presumably was no more. But to take any action in the legislature he first had to be duly certified as Mansfield's representative to get a seat there. Initial action on this was promising but after various committee and floor maneuverings in the House his bid for recognition died a quiet death. For Luce — now a town representative without a town — it was a pretty ignominious defeat.

He did not, however, let the matter rest there. According to Bigelow, "as a test case, a suit for trespass was brought by him against the constable of the town of Stowe who had taken some property belonging to one of Mr. Luce's sons who had refused to pay his taxes on it assessed by the town of Stowe. The case was carried to the Supreme Court of the state which decided that the act of annexation was constitutional." And, Bigelow continues, "it is related that at one of the meetings where the matter was being discussed, Mr. Luce became so violently angry at Elisha Town, also a resident of Mansfield, but who had voted for the annexation, that he went about with a knife in his hand looking for Mr. Town and saying 'I'll have his heart's blood!' " That Ivory was so up in arms was probably a *good* thing for Town since he "was in a wagon nearby but Mr. Luce was too excited to see him."

Ivory's efforts on the annexation matter apparently did carry a measure of success for in 1853 the legislature acted again. This time it repealed the act of 1848 subject to the reorganization of Mansfield and approval of the repeal by both towns, that is, Stowe and Mansfield. But none of these necessary actions ever occurred. Earlier Ivory had won a small victory in some other litigation with the town of Stowe involving the annexation issue. But his personal war, after some 23 years, had been lost.

One historic footnote to the annexation of Mansfield to its neighboring towns of Stowe and Underhill carries an element of mystery, more on which will be noted in Chapter 11. It might only be noted here that the present boundary line between the latter two towns makes a zig-zag across the ridge line of Mt. Mansfield. The zig includes the Forehead and Nose in Stowe while the zag includes the Chin, which is the highest part of the mountain, in Underhill. In subsequent years it has been Stowe which has dominated the recreational development of the mountain and in this way has more or less laid claim to the whole mountain. But it remains that the summit, the highest point of land in the state, actually lies in Underhill.

Ivory Luce did not depart the Mansfield scene as he had in such a fury from Hartland but continued to work the 500 or more acres which he had cleared on his namesake hill. These eventually became individual farms for five of his sons. He was 88 years old when he died on April 21, 1870. In compliance with his request he was buried on Luce Hill and his stone may still be seen in the small family cemetery there.

This man, his times and the town he had helped settle and tried to preserve are all touched on in a poem which appeared not long after Ivory's death. This deals with one 'Lish Brown which later authorities have recognized as Ivory Luce. The poem's story is said to be "literally true."

'LISH BROWN — A REMINISCENCE

By S.S. Luce

Two score years ago, in a New England town,
There lived an "odd stick" by the name of 'Lish Brown.
That's what the boys called him, and seldom you find,
A man so peculiar in mind.

He was coarse in his manners, he stooped in his gait,
With arms like gorilla's a tough curly pate;
But what struck a stranger with wonder complete,
Were his pedals—O, weren't they the marvel of feet!
He lived on a hill, in a town very new,
Where the bears were in plenty, the citizens few,
And 'tis said that he often, in combat had pressed
Old bruin, who always came off second best....

To return to our subject—Mr. Brown,
Who lived in a bit of a New England town
Where all might, with hope, to an office aspire,
For the least in the place wasn't less than a squire:—
Thus it chanced that our hero, one fine autumn day,
To a seat in the Assembly was making his way;
His toilet I'm told, was his all and his best:
Straw hat and tow pants, without coat or vest,
The distance was twenty five miles, made on foot,
With feet that were guiltless of shoe or of boot,

Arrived at the Capitol, where he took seat
With members in broadcloth that co'dn't be beat.
Some shrank from his touch, as they would from a snake,
Exclaimed in disgust, "There's sure some mistake!"
While others inclined to be waggish and smart,
Most knowingly winked brother members apart;
One said: "Mr. Brown, I hope not to offend,
But had your town no one quite proper to send?"
Said Brown: "There's plenty that's better I s'pose,
But stranger, the fact is, they hadn't got clothes."

CHAPTER
4

Joints and Other Geology

MYTHOLOGY AND SCIENCE are like oil and water — they don't mix so good. Four legends of how Mt. Mansfield was formed were described in the opening chapter. The true believer will do well to skip what follows for here we shall let science take the podium with its account of our mountain's origins and evolution.

Strictly speaking the geologic history of the Mansfield area goes back to the beginnings of the earth itself. We shall promptly forget the first several billions of years and content ourselves with only the more "recent" hundreds of millions years. Even this part of the story is a complex one, the threads of which geologists are still trying to sort out, and any summary of it runs the risk of over-simplification.

Earlier epochs in which mountains were formed, worn down and covered over by the ocean left vast layers of sedimentary rock in what is now Vermont and New Hampshire. Great pressure and heat wrought changes in the structure and chemistry of this rock, forming it into what is known as metamorphic rock. Also at play was the force of the earth's gravity drawing our globe into an ever-smaller mass; the result was a wrinkling of the earth's surface into a series of folds like the skin of a dried apple. The resulting upheaval left the progenitors of the present Green and White Mountains. Those first ranges were much higher than what exists today, probably 5,000 feet higher and perhaps more.

For the main Green Mountain range another factor was at work. This was a massive lateral thrust which shifted some of the older strata in a northwesterly direction up and over the younger strata. Subsequent to these basic formative forces, lesser uplifts and movements further altered the major outlines of our mountain and the range of which it is a part.

The metamorphic bedrock of Mansfield is estimated to be about 380 millions of years old. The first folding and elevation of this and the original, younger strata of rock above it are said to have taken place some 350 million years ago. The younger strata since then have been eroded away.

Compared to these time spans, the last major phenomenon to affect Mansfield happened like only yesterday. This was the Pleistocene or Ice Age when large continental glaciers advanced and retreated several times through New England and elsewhere with the last big melt occurring "only" some 12,000 years ago.

The most explicit evidence of the existence, depth and movement of the ice sheet across Mansfield takes two forms. One is the grooves or "striae" in the bedrock; these are marked gouges caused by boulders embedded in the base or sole of the glacier. The other is glacial "erratics" which are boulders and smaller stones, particularly those of non-indigenous material, which have been picked up and carried by the ice sheet and then deposited in a new location when the ice melted. Of particular interest are two of these "drift rocks" on the summit ridge just south of the Upper Lip. Glacial striae pass beneath the boulders indicating that they were not at their present position when the striae were formed. The rocks are believed to have been deposited by an ice sheet though their original location may have been only a short distance away; they may even have been the very stones which caused the underlying glacial scratches.

One drift rock left on Mansfield is no longer there. This five-foot boulder is a specimen of a coarse syenite or Labradorite, a mineral material definitely of foreign origins. Geologists have pinpointed its probable place of origin as some 120 miles northwest of Montreal, the nearest location of bedrock of similar character. The egg-shaped boulder, weighing more than three tons, was originally found near the Toll Road about a mile and a half below the summit. On May 13, 1921 it was brought down the mountain to the River Bank Cemetery near Stowe village and, as part of the town's Memorial Day ceremonies that year, was dedicated by the local chapter of the Women's Relief Corps as a war memorial with the following inscription: "To Our Defenders — 1775-1918 — Past, Present, Future."

Of this rock's unnatural drift to the valley below at least one man was not very happy. State Geologist Elbridge C. Jacobs some years later wrote: "It had better have been left where it was a true memorial of the ice age."

One other interesting question is whether or not local glaciers — as distinguished from the all-encompassing continental ice sheet — ever wound their way down Mansfield's slopes. Contemrorary geologists generally concur with their predecessor, James Walter Goldthwait, who in a 1915-16 report cited "a complete absence of records" of local glaciers on any of the higher Green Mountains. One geologist, however, has recently modified this view somewhat to the effect that if there had never been a full-grown glacier on Mansfield there at least had been accumulations of heavy-packed granular snow sufficient to have modified the mountain's terrain in some areas.

One other geologic feature of our mountain which bears mention is its so-called "joints" (not to be confused, as one jocular geologist noted, with establishments dispensing alcoholic beverages). These are fractures in a rock mass where the continuity of each stratum across the break has not been disturbed. They have been likened to a pack of playing cards which has been cut in one or more places. Where the strata are still touching they are called "closed joints," and where separated, "open joints."

Many of Mansfield's interesting rock formations are joints. Several are found along the Maple Ridge Trail including one notable for its four-foot width and the length and straightness of the break. The Subway and Wall Street Trails carry one through other open joints. A joint of special note is the Cave of the Winds which will be described in more detail in Chapter 6.

No minerals or metals of great economic value have been found on Mansfield though Underhill residents report that a group of men once opened up a large pit on that side of the mountain where evidence of an iron deposit had been found. But the richness of the deposit proved insufficient to merit commercial mining. Some flecks of gold have also been found but there has never been a Mansfield Gold Rush.

How Smuggler's Notch was formed is still a matter of some uncertainty for geologists. The simplest explanation would be that Mansfield and Sterling Mountains were once united and that, as one 19th century chronicler put it, "by some mighty convulsion or upheaving of the earth, they were separated." But geologists find no evidence of such a momentous event and instead attribute the Notch's formation to the perhaps more prosaic, and certainly far slower, action of glaciers and running water.

To begin with the ridge once connecting the Mansfield-Sterling massifs is said to have been an "anticline", the downfolding strata of which are more subject to erosion. Prior to the Ice Age the action of water first opened a gap in the ridge. Tongues of ice from the continental glaciers are believed to have moved through this gap and reshaped it to some extent.

It was in the aftermath of the Ice Age that geologists conjecture the major erosion of the Notch occurred. The present two small streams flowing out of the pass are not nearly large enough to account for the massive cut. This could only have been done by a much larger volume of water and the source for this, geologists suggest, was the massive continental glaciers themselves. As they picture it, an ice sheet retreated first from the narrower valley on the east side of the range leaving a still-standing wall of ice on the west side. Run-off from this produced the great volume of water which wore its way through the Notch, slowly deepening it with each passing year.

So in large measure it has been the long-term effects of erosion by water and ice which have worn down Mansfield from its far loftier mass and carved out the impressive Smuggler's Notch. When one visits the mountain or Notch time stands still and it's hard to imagine that the leveling process still goes on. But of course it does.

On a day in May of 1969 the winter snows had finally melted from Rt. 108 through the Notch and the road opened for summer travel. The skies also opened, leaving some three inches of rain on the mountain. Up on the Mansfield side of the Notch the ground gave way and tons of rock, mud and trees plummeted down the steep slope, blocking off the road and leaving a gash in the mountainside which is still very evident. That was the most recent landslide on the mountain, one of nature's more dramatic phenomena of erosion. There have been a number of other slides, all on the west and north sides of Mansfield.

The earliest of which there is record occurred on July 27, 1833. Another landslide occurred on the Cambridge side in 1848; this ran nearly three miles from the Chin to the mountain's base. A landslide in 1887 has been perhaps the most dramatic in human terms but before providing details on that other slides might be noted here for the record. One occurred on August 11, 1892 which was described as "40 rods wide and nearly a mile in length." Following heavy rains in August, 1955 the ground gave way just above the Mt. Mansfield State Forest Campground in Underhill. And on May 24 or 25, 1966 a rock slide occurred in the Notch. This by itself did not close the road but enough of the boulders were hanging so precariously above it that traffic was halted until they could be cleared away.

On Friday, June 3, 1887, the day dawned dull and overcast. John Flynn was an Underhill farmer who lived at the base of Mansfield with his wife and their seven children. He found himself extremely uneasy and when his wife inquired about his restlessness he explained that he had a premonition that some bad weather was on its way. Hardly had he spoken when the skies opened in a long-lasting downpour. Then, according to one account, as the family huddled inside their home "the whole mountain reverberated with a terrible crash and roar; the mighty roar of waters increased and giant trees torn from their roots passed by making them believe each moment would be their last."

Stunned with horror, Flynn and his family fell on their knees in prayer. The storm continued but the house held firm. Then the rain finally subsided and they were able to go outside. "What a spectacle met their eyes!," our chronicler continues. "For it seemed as if the whole mountain side had slid down. Standing on their sides and protruding from the vast accumulation of earth were trees fifty to eighty feet in length and from one to three feet in diameter which had been hurled down the mountain like corn cobs, while vast rocks weighing from one to five hundred tons had been hurled about like baseballs. . ."

The scene was appalling but the family also saw what for them was the miracle which had spared their home and themselves. With the first rush of debris a natural dam had been created just above the house causing the water and landslide to go around the building. "And John Flynn to the end of his days remembered this miracle and thanked God by the life he lived."

Other residents of the affected area somehow managed to have a sense of humor about the whole thing. The *News and Citizen* of Hyde Park reported that "Henry Brush says he would give $500 and L. Dickinson $200 if their farms could be put back where they were last Friday morning." The *Burlington Free Press and Times* gave an estimate of the slide's proportions as two miles long, 100 to 600 feet wide and 20 to 40 feet deep (this gash in Mansfield's flank is still visible). That the slide was a major event was reflected in the *Free Press* report that "hundreds of people are visiting the scene daily."

Note has already been made of the large rock removed from Mansfield's summit area to a new resting place in the Stowe valley. A second rock of some note was brought from the scene of this landslide by one of those visitors.

The rock is not a large one — about 14 inches long and 29 inches in circumference. But it is notable for its even shape, like an oversize football, and for its weight, an estimated 75 pounds which for its size seems pretty hefty. It was these features in any event which attracted Ben Safford of Cambridge to lug the stone back home from the landslide debris where he had found it. What gives the stone additional special interest is the unusual attachment which the man came to have for it. His nephew, John Safford, who now has the stone, tells the story: "He carried it everywhere with him. I guess he was afraid somebody would steal it. Ben even took it to Florida and back on one trip."

And so nature has built up and worn down our mountain. But there is quite a bit of it left and in the next chapter we shall take a look at just how big that "bit" is.

CHAPTER 5

Mountain Height and Mountain Pride

... It is not likely that the health or comfort of many persons depend on knowing which is the highest of the Vermont mountains....

THIS APPROPRIATE REMARK was made by the editor of the *Burlington Free Press and Times* in 1901. It appeared in a story on various claims and counterclaims regarding the heights of certain of the Green Mountains, notably Mt. Mansfield, Camel's Hump and Killington Mountain.

While the report included this apologetic comment on the whole issue, the editor had proceeded to take several other newspapers to task for their publication of allegedly erroneous information on the matter and concluded by presenting other evidence that he hoped would establish once and for all that Mansfield was the state's highest mountain. It is indeed the loftiest summit of Vermont but it was some years after this little journalistic fol-de-rol that very precise measurements of the different mountain altitudes in question finally confirmed the fact.

The establishment of Mt. Mansfield as Vermont's highest peak is a story woven of two basic threads. One is the technical tale of the various measurements of the mountain's altitude, at least nine of which have been made over the years. The second is the thread of competition within the state in which Mansfield's height has been compared to that of other prominent mountains. Ours may indeed now rank as Vermont's highest but at one point promoters of other peaks had dropped it not only to second place but to third.

Hypsometry is the term given to the science of land altitude measurements and there are basically four ways of finding the height of a specific piece of terrain. A very approximate method is by determining the boiling point of water at the elevation in question. The temperature at which liquid water turns to vapor decreases with a reduction in air pressure and air pressure decreases as altitude increases. Thus somebody at the top of a mountain of unknown altitude can, by measuring the temperature of boiling water at that point, get an approximation of the mountain height by comparing this temperature to a table of boiling points previously determined for known altitudes.

The other three methods have been the ones generally used by surveyors. Roughly speaking, the complexity and cost of these several techniques goes up in proportion to their preciseness of results. The simplest is the use of a barometer for measuring air pressure which, as noted, decreases as altitude increases. By relating the air pressure at a previously fixed lower elevation to that of an unmeasured summit, the altitude of the latter can be determined. The next more precise method is by trigonometric or angular measurement. This involves more complex equipment. By starting at points of known elevation the altitude of a distant peak can be calculated by using assorted sines and cosines of trigonometry.

The most precise method of determining land altitudes, and also the most involved, is the use of the spirit level, an instrument with one of those little bubbles floating around in it. There are several degrees of refinement in this method but the procedure involved is basically the same. As a series of lines is run from a beginning point of known altitude, the change in elevation between each two of the successive points is precisely determined using the level and a vertical measuring rod. These step-by-step increments (and some will be plus and others minus) are totalled up when the summit is reached to get the final change in altitude between the starting and ending points.

The first measurement of Mt. Mansfield's height was made in 1818 by a Capt. Alden Partridge who left an interesting account of his trip. Partridge, a professor of engineering, came to Vermont from New York City with a view to making "physical and barometrical observations" of Mansfield and Camel's Hump, or Camel's Rump as it was then wryly being called. He succeeded in both and in the process walked and climbed some 72 miles in a three-day period, most of it in soaking rain. His results were: for Camel's Hump, 4,188 feet, and for Mt. Mansfield, 4,279 feet.

Settlers in the Waterbury-Stowe area were already comparing these two mountains, which are in sight of each other, and sizing up which was the loftier. An article in the July 2, 1873 issue of the *Lamoille Newsdealer* of Hyde Park takes note of this competition and provides a delightful anecdote as to how the question was settled:

> In an "airly day" before the science of engineering was used in this vicinity, a dispute arose among the hunters as to the relative heighths of Mansfield and Camel's Hump, — each mountain being claimed as the highest by their respective champions. To settle the matter an old hunter took his long smooth-bore rifle, and went to the top of Mansfield, placed a small ball in the rifle, which was level-sighted, then aimed it directly at the top of Camel's Hump. The ball rolled out of the rifle and Old Mansfield was declared the higher mountain.

Sometime between 1824 and 1842 a civil engineer named Edwin F. Johnson figured Mansfield's height to be 4,359 feet by a trigonometrical measurement. In 1848 or shortly before, Zadock Thompson, our gazetteer compiler, determined it was 4,348 feet high, making his own measurement with a barometer. Two men calculated its altitude in 1857: Dr. Edward Hitchcock, a geologist, found the summit to be 4,329 feet high while Professor A. Guyot of Princeton College came up with (or, more literally, went down with) a figure of 4,430 feet. Both of these were also barometric measurements.

In 1864, the first application of the leveling method to Mansfield was made by H. Doton of Pomfret, Vermont. His result was 4,389.08 feet. That this figure is only four feet short of the 4,393.3 feet that is the present official altitude of our mountain is creditable enough. What is surprising is that it subsequently received very little attention, despite the preciseness of the method used. It's too bad for as we shall shortly see it probably would have prevented callouses on a few editors' fingers.

In the meantime other figures appeared. A large map of Vermont published in 1893 by J.L. Beers & Co. identifies Mansfield as 4,278 feet high. And in 1895 the *Boston Home Journal* carried an article reporting the altitude as 4,457 feet. No source for the last figure was given. This is a little unfortunate as it does represent the very highest reach into the clouds that surveyors and other technicians, at least, have ever given to our mountain. Promoters of the top of Mansfield had a slightly different view of things, however.

Neither of the last-mentioned measurements nor any of the earlier or subsequent figures are above 4,500 feet, at which point mathematical rules technically would permit a rounding to a nice fat 5,000 feet. This, however, did not deter the managers of the Summit House on Mt. Mansfield, a seasonal hostelry located just below the Nose. Sometime in the late 1800's they put out a promotional broadside on their facilities proclaiming "Mansfield Mountain is the highest land in the State and is about 5,000 Feet High ..." That figure was in big bold letters on a separate line.

All during this time measurements were being made of other Vermont peaks as well. Of these, Camel's Hump and Killington Mountain, which lies well south in Sherburne, figured most prominently in the regional competition which emerged from time to time over who had the highest mountain. Up to this point, Killington and the Hump each could be shown, depending on which figures one cited, to be second highest to Mansfield. But the latter was generally conceded to be the loftiest.

It was in the early 1890's that Killington backers latched onto new evidence which appeared to show that their mountain was the state's highest. What happened was that the U.S. Coast and Geodetic Survey about this time set up surveying stations on the two mountains and subsequently announced their measurements of the altitudes of the two points — 4,241 feet for Killington and 4,071 feet for the Mansfield station. But that makes Killington higher than Mansfield! Exactly, and that's just what many gathered from the figures.

What had happened was that the Geodetic Survey had stationed itself on the summit of Killington but for Mansfield had located its survey point *not* on the summit (the Chin) but on the Nose, which is several hundred feet lower. These respective station points were identified with the altitudes given out but, as the *Burlington Free Press and Times* reported in an 1897 issue, "Being ignorant of, or overlooking [these facts] ... many persons at once jumped to the conclusion that the Geodetic survey had upset all the previous measurements of the two mountains and that Killington was now proved to be the highest of the Green Mountains."

Thus we have arrived in 1901 in which year Mansfield was momentarily dethroned again and tumbled not just to second place but to third. The scramble in the mountain peak pecking order began with the *Middlebury Register* which reported that a recently discovered government survey carried out by a Professor Raphael Pompilly showed that Camel's Hump was higher than Mansfield. The *Free Press* promptly countered by citing *published* government figures which listed Mansfield as the highest, Killington as second highest and Camel's Hump as third. (By now, still another measurement of Mansfield's altitude put it at 4,364 feet.)

At this point the *News* of Rutland, which city lies in Killington's back yard, came out with the following:

> Mount Mansfield has been standing many years under false pretenses. It has been carrying the reputation of being the highest peak in Vermont's Green Mountains. More accurate surveys made Killington higher than Mansfield,* although it seems difficult for Mansfield to give up the reputation it has so long borne. And now comes Camel's Hump which, according to Professor Pompilly, who made the latest and most accurate governmental survey, is 35 feet higher than Mansfield. Thus Mansfield becomes the third highest peak in the state.

Hardly about to turn his cheek, the *Free Press* editor, G.G. Benedict, tried first to discredit

---

*This is a reference to that Geodetic Survey of the early 1890's involving the misleading figure for Mansfield's Nose.

the attribution to Pompilly by writing him direct. The Professor responded with a little buck-passing and Benedict eventually received from a federal agency the same official figures he already had in hand. These were: Mt. Mansfield, 4,364 feet; Killington Peak, 4,241 feet; and Camel's Hump, 4,088 feet. "We submit," asserted the *Free Press* spokesman, "that this ought to settle the question if it has ever been unsettled." Then in an effort to diminish the sound and fury he went on: "It is not likely that the health or comfort of many persons depend on knowing which is the highest of the Vermont mountains. But . . . if it is worthwhile to say anything on the subject it is worthwhile to state the truth."

To all this the *News and Citizen* of Hyde Park responded with a blast of braggadocio for Lamoille County (despite the fact that Mansfield's summit, as we have seen, is not in that county but Chittenden). Opening with a terse "Of course it is!", long-time editor L. H. Lewis then goes on:

> . . . The *Burlington Free Press* has produced statistics and figures that prove "beyond a doubt" that Mt. Mansfield is the highest point of the Green Mountains. We long ago knew this was true and hope now that official figures are given those fellows who have been yawping about Killington Peak, Camel's Hump and other diminutive points will let up and not only remember that Mt. Mansfield is the highest point, but that Lamoille County, in which old Mansfield is located, is the best county in the state.

That seemed to do it. Nary another peep was heard about those "other diminutive points." Mansfield had regained its title and no challenge has since been made.

It was not until 1924, however, that the final, and now present, official altitude was measured. The U.S. Geological Survey in that year ran a level survey of Mansfield which showed the mountain's altitude to be that 4,393.3 feet mentioned earlier. A copper disc was cemented into the very top of the Chin in which this figure was inscribed. This is still in place.

The *Free Press and Times* carried a story about the measurement which, it said, had been checked "from the opposite direction with a variation of but .001 feet." That and "final" measurements of the other prominent Green Mountains now leave the following rank order behind (or below) Mansfield: Killington second at 4,235 feet, Mt. Ellen in Warren (a newcomer), third at 4,135 feet, and Camel's Hump fourth at 4,083 feet.

Old Mansfield, as our report on its geology has shown, is indeed well along in years. As the human form shrinks with age, so that craggy chin may have been weathered down to 4,393.2 feet since 1924. But it still stands tallest in Vermont's Green Mountains.

CHAPTER 6

Features

Following this outline from the south, a graceful curve describes what phrenologists would call a rather handsome forehead, with a full medium amount of brain. The same outline continues, until it presents the appearance of a very well formed Nose, belonging decidedly to the class called "Pug." Then follows a level space, reaching two considerable hills, which well represent the Lips. About this region however is a slight depression, which in similar instances has been greatly improved by an artificial set of teeth. Still further on the outline is completed by another high elevation forming a very well shaped chin.

MAN HAS LONG DELIGHTED in finding his own image projected in natural features around him and this was the description of Mansfield's famous profile which a chronicler identified only as "T.M.M." provided back in 1870. It is fairly typical of the verbal anthropomorphic renderings of our mountain which visitors in the latter 19th century seemed to enjoy creating. Area residents and visitors in more recent years seem less given to this sort of thing though the individual names for the mountain man's features — Forehead, Nose, Upper and Lower Lips and Chin — remain firmly fixed in use.

The identification of these features has been carried even further. North of the Chin is another prominence called the Adam's Apple. Of the Cave of the Winds, of which more shortly, T.M.M. wrote, "Whether this opening be the path to the Old Man's stomach has not been determined. Thankful not to be swallowed by the giant, visitors are glad to leave this chilling cavern believing the Old Man's heart to be as cold as stone." A cave on the Nose has been likened to a Nostril and there's even an Eyebrow on the Forehead.

As for the human qualities found in the complete profile, T.M.M.'s description, despite the prescription of false teeth, was a fairly flattering one. Several others have been something less than that. Wrote Gay H. Naramore in 1857: "Mansfield's forehead is not very intellectual — his chin, like that of many others, being the highest. He has a regular cave of a mouth, terribly twisted, [which] opens down on the north-east side, yawning and awful, with a breath that strikes a blight like that of angry winter." Ah, but the Nose! That "is not Roman," according to Naramore, "... but a right Yankee sneezer three hundred feet high." And Vermont Geologist Albert D. Hager provided this character analysis in 1861:

When the fact is stated that the Chin is the highest point of land in Vermont, it might be conjectured by those who never saw the mountain that the profile is ill shaped and disproportionate; for if it were not the profile of an idiot it might be inferred that the forehead or nose would be higher than the chin.

Another 19th century writer, identified only as "N.W.G.," joins Hager in a satisfying explanation of the elevated Chin; this simply shows "that the old man's pillow was too low when he lay down, or that he threw up his chin before going to sleep, as some people are in the habit of doing, for the convenience of breathing or snoring."

The Cave of the Winds, alluded to here as the mountain man's gut, is one of Mansfield's features which for some years has held fascination for explorers. The earliest record of a probe into the deep cleft found by the writer was that in a newspaper account of 1853. A party of four using a rope climbed to a point part way down; here they threw rocks into the cave's ice-coated depths. But they re-ascended without going further.

What was claimed as the cave's first complete exploration occurred in early September, 1911 and was described in some detail in a local newspaper account. The six men involved in the adventure entered the cave and moving a short ways down a steep slope came to where a large rock is wedged between the cave walls — the deepest point to which earlier explorers had gone. Here using ropes and flashlights they continued the descent to the bottom, a total depth which they estimated at 120 feet. They also found ice which for the time of year in which the descent was made suggested this was to be found in the cave year-round. There was also this interesting note: "A current of air can be felt in the cave and it is believed that there is another opening which may be the small aperture found farther down the mountainside. The cave narrows so small, however, that the only possible entrance and exit is the one opening used." Exploration of the Cave of the Winds, the report concluded, "requires a cool head and steady nerves. It is not a cave to be visited often or by large numbers of people."

Other descents have been made since that time and the later installation of a ladder eased part of the descent. This, however, has recently been removed. Parties still make the descent with ropes but caution is very much in order for any new potential explorers of this exciting Mansfield feature.

Note was made in Chapter 4 of the two glacial drift rocks located just south of the Upper Lip. Several other stones of special interest are — or once were — found along the summit ridge. One that now belongs to the past is a mammoth boulder estimated to weigh 1,000 tons which for time unknown had stood delicately poised on the top of the Nose, defying, according to one account, "the elements, the boys, and numerous quantities of gunpowder" which had affected or sought to affect its balance. On July 4, 1856 twenty-five pounds of gunpowder had been fired under it "which loosened it somewhat from its moorings." Then on August 14 the stone's remaining props gave way of their own accord and down it plunged, smashing into fragments at the base of the Nose.

One reason for the efforts to dislodge the boulder had been local concern about visitors' insistence on climbing over it despite warnings of its precarious position — as many as thirty persons were said to have been on it at one time. As it happened no luckless human was atop the stone when it did fall. But just twenty minutes earlier somebody had been there — a Mr. and Mrs. J.A.S. White of Northfield and their daughter; they were already part way down the mountain when the big rock fell. The concussion, according to White, was like an earthquake — "it shook the whole mountain." White and his family were also undoubtedly shaken a bit by their narrow escape.

Several so-called Balance Rocks remain, however. One notable one, some six or eight feet in size, hangs precariously over a sharp drop-off on the east side of the Upper

Lip. Just above this at the top of a vertical ledge is a dramatic crag which has been known as the Rock of Terror. Other related features of the summit area include Hambone's Crater, a table-sized gouge in the rock on the south side of the Chin left there when lightning struck the spot a couple of years ago; large fragments of stone from the "explosion" are scattered nearby. This feature was named after its discoverer, Hamilton "Hambone" Strayer, a Mt. Mansfield Co. employe. Also on the Chin is a profile dubbed The Turtle; a couple of stones form the head and open mouth of the creature. On the east side of the Nose a human likeness is outlined against the sky which in oldtime descriptive accounts has been called the "Old Man of Mansfield."

But the mountain's stone of stones is undoubtedly Cantilever Rock. This is a great shaft 39 feet long and weighing an estimated 75 tons which stands, or rather lies, at nearly a right angle to an open cliff wall on the lower west side of the mountain. Its base is wedged under an outcropping of the cliff and is overlaid by just a few inches of jutting stone. For nine feet the shaft's lower edge rests on another outcropping; beyond this it extends unsupported for 30 feet, tapering to about 17 inches at its end. The overall appearance is thus a cantilevered one which gives the impressive stone its name.

Somewhat surprisingly, the world learned of this natural oddity only a few short years ago. In June, 1960 Clyde H. Smith, then of South Burlington and now of Shelburne, and his father, Clyde F. Smith, were rambling on Mansfield off the beaten track. "At a point going up near a big rock 'chimney'," the younger Smith told a *Burlington Free Press* reporter several months later, "I climbed a small rock pedestal, and looking down saw this tremendous obelisk some 300 feet away, extending from the face of the cliff, nearly concealed by trees. I couldn't believe my eyes." Accompanying the news story was a photograph of the stone with Smith standing at its very end, a point he had reached using ropes as a safety measure.

On one of his return visits to take careful measurements of the unusual find Smith made an additional discovery: on the ground below is a four-foot rock, now moss-covered, which clearly seems to have been the original tip end of the overhanging rock. This, he told the writer, presumably fell off sometime after Cantilever Rock had slipped into its present position. At the time of his discovery Smith also checked with several persons very familiar with the mountain but none knew of any earlier sighting of the big stone. On that basis, the *Free Press* report had noted, "It is quite probable ... that due to its obscure location, no man has ever before violated the great obelisk's dignified location. Certainly it has never before been photographed."

The fact is, however, that 29 years earlier another man had not only seen the unusual stone but had photographed it as well. The man was Huntley Palmer who now lives in retirement near Montpelier Junction. In October, 1931, he told the writer, he came across the rock while working over this area of Mt. Mansfield mapping types of forest growth for the Vermont Forest Service. The oddity struck him sufficiently to go back the next day with his camera for a picture of it but, as he put it, "I didn't think anything more about it and don't make any claim about being its first discoverer. But I was there."

Cantilever Rock in any event is now very much in the public domain with a trail leading to it and hundreds of visitors trekking up for a view each year; for many the first reaction to the great stone and its precarious position is like that of "discoverer" Smith: "I can't believe it."

One of Mansfield's most idyllic features is tiny, crescent-shaped Lake of the Clouds. The body of water, only a couple of acres in size and but four or five feet at its deepest, lies a short ways below the steep north face of the Chin. The pond has no inlet as such — water run-off from the surrounding slopes keeps it replenished — but its outlet is Hell's Brook which makes a steep run down into Smuggler's Notch. The lake's elevation is just under 4,000 feet which makes it the highest body of water in the state. It also represents one of Vermont's most isolated ponds — the steep trek down from the Chin discourages many from visiting it — and as such its pristine condition holds a special charm for those who have reached its spruce and balsam shoreline.

The name, Lake of the Clouds, has been used for well over a hundred years but who first called it that is unknown. Back in 1860, however, a group of visitors including no less than University of Vermont President Calvin Pease carried out a little ceremony formally rechristening it Crescent Lake. Their principal reason for the change was the existence of another tarn of the same name high in the White Mountains. (The New Hampshire Lake of the Clouds, which is the highest body of water on the eastern seaboard, is located between Mts. Monroe and Washington.) But tradition has outweighed ceremony; the new name for Mansfield's lake was soon forgotten and the original has remained in use.

Two other bodies of water are associated with our mountain. One is Bear Pond, an oversized puddle located a half-mile down the mountain from the Lake of the Clouds. The source of this name is also lost but it, too, had a different identification at one time. Engineer D.C. Linsley of Burlington, who in 1866 surveyed the route for a proposed toll road up the Cambridge-Underhill side of Mansfield, named it Eagle Lake after several of these majestic birds which he saw flying over it.

The other is Lake Mansfield at the base of the mountain's southern end near Nebraska Notch. It is a 40-acre artificial lake which is the home of the Lake Mansfield Trout Club. The club was organized by several Stowe men in 1899 and the dam built in 1900 (the story goes that inspiration for the lake's location came to the club's later first president, Orlo E. Luce, as he surveyed the area from the top of a tree where an angry bull had chased him). The lake has been regularly stocked with trout and a clubhouse and related facilities have been added over the years on the shore of this very picturesque lake.

Another aquatic feature of special interest in the mountain's immediate area is Bingham Falls on Notch Brook in Stowe. This is a beautiful cascade at the end of a long cut which the stream makes through solid rock. The falls were named after W.H.H. Bingham, a lawyer who played a prominent role in the development of Stowe's early tourist facilities. A trail to the stream and falls leaves Rt. 108 a short ways above the Lodge at Smuggler's Notch.

Note was made in Chapter 1 of how Mt. Mansfield's appearance signals changes in weather and in the final chapter other information on our mountain's weather will be provided. But this chapter seems an appropriate place for details of an unusual phenomenon which was witnessed from the summit ridge in 1863. This was experienced by a man identified only as "B." and his companions. According to the account which B. sent to a Burlington newspaper, his party was viewing Smuggler's Notch from an overlook north of Mansfield's Chin. A strong wind was swirling cloud masses through the Notch from the Stowe side and the sun was lighting them up as they moved along the west side of Sterling Mountain. B.'s account continues:

> Suddenly, we saw a heavy, dense, dark cloud of mist coming up the valley ... When the rays of the sun struck it, as it passed along opposite to us, we saw, as if by magic, in the midst of the cloud and very near to us, a circle of the most vivid colors, about 30 feet in diameter, and in the center of this immense picture frame our own images were distinctly photographed. We had time to change our positions, throw our arms about, and toss up our hats, and watch the same performance by the dumb imitators in the cloud. We went wild with excitement at the glorious scene, and we were sorry that it did not "hold on," for it lasted but little more than a minute. After waiting some time, the "fog circle" with

its brilliant colors was repeated, but our pictures were left out.

Personnel at the WCAX Television transmitter station at the top of the mountain told the writer they had seen phenomena similar to this though none just like it.

The final feature of Mt. Mansfield of special note is nothing of the mountain itself but rather the magnificent views of everything else around it. Off to the west is Lake Champlain and New York State's Adirondacks beyond; to the east, the Stowe valley and Worcester Range in the near distance and the White Mountains in the background; and to the north and south the flow of the other Green Mountains.

The writer will not even begin to list other prominent individual mountains which can be seen from the summit ridge. Rather he will pay homage to a man who was undoubtedly Mansfield's champion mountain-spotter, the late Harold P. Frost of Worcester, Mass. Frost built a crude but reasonably accurate compass device which he would mount on the porch of the Summit House for locating and identifying individual mountains. By 1953, when Frost described his hobby of some seven years for the Green Mountain Club's *Long Trail News,* he had charted 60 different mountains by name and angle. The farthest mountain positively identified was 83 miles away though Frost does not state which one that was. Many of these mountains he and his wife had climbed, some of them several times. So he was far from merely a porch-bound amateur surveyor but an avid hiker as well.

What happened to Frost's Mountain-Spotter and the chart which he compiled is not known (he died in 1955). But as for the Summit House and the porch on which he had set it up, that definitely is no more. This famous little hostelry will be the subject of a later chapter. But for the moment we shall leave Mt. Mansfield itself and explore that dramatic and interesting mountain gap to its immediate north, Smuggler's Notch.

STAINED GLASS — A view of Mt. Mansfield from the town of Westford is rendered in this Tiffany stained glass window at the Proctor Union Church in Proctor, Vt. Westford was the childhood home of Mrs. Minnie E. Proctor in whose memory the window was dedicated.

Photo by the Author

SKIING COW — Principals connected with Stowe's Mansfield Dairy and the famous skiing cow trademark used on its milk containers and delivery trucks are: at center, Mrs. Dorothy Nelson, originator of the figure in 1939; at left, Carroll Pike, long-time operator and still owner of the dairy; and at right, Winford Small, who currently leases the business from Pike.

Photo by the Author

DRIFT ROCK MEMORIAL — This rock which was originally left near the summit of Mt. Mansfield by an Ice Age glacier was brought to the River Bank Cemetery in Stowe in 1921 where it has since served as a veterans memorial.

Photo by the Author

Stowe Reporter

SUMMIT FEATURES — Don Bowley, above, a Vermont Forests and Parks Department warden, stands atop the so-called Rock of Terror on Mansfield's summit ridge; in background is the Nose and its several television antenna towers. At left, Toby Elliman of Stowe with the help of a ladder and the cable above climbs through one of the dramatic crevices along the Canyon-Subway connecting trails just over the west side of the ridge.

CANTILEVER ROCK — Clyde H. Smith, a discoverer in 1960 of this natural oddity on the west side of Mansfield, stands near the end of its nearly 40-foot length — a practice he does not recommend without safety ropes. Below is a photo by Huntley Palmer taken when he came across the unusual formation in 1931.

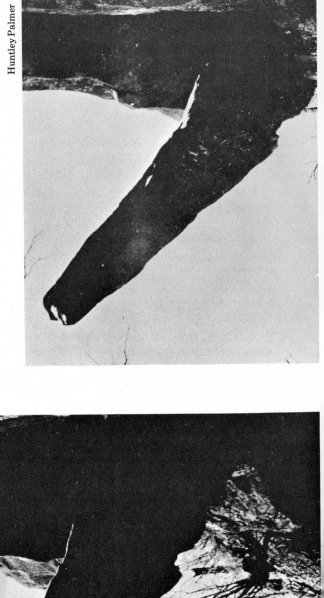

Huntley Palmer

Clyde F. Smith

ELEPHANT'S HEAD — At right, this well-known feature of Smuggler's Notch as it appeared some years ago; in 1964 a major portion of the trunk's right side departed the head. Below, Lewis Coty and Chris Curtis, two Stowe youths, are pictured at a point in their successful climb of the Head, only the second time it has been done.

Courtesy — Mrs. Blanche Sanborn
© Harry Richardson — Used by permission

Joel Anderson

BIG SPRING - SMUGGLERS NOTCH - VERMONT

STAFFORD PHOTO

C.C. Stafford

NOTCH FEATURES — Above is the notable Big Spring of Smuggler's Notch as it appeared probably in the 1930's after concrete "tank" and rock walls had been built around it. The sign reads: "Put Cups In Refuse Can/Water 99% Pure — 39 Deg." The spring today has reverted in large measure to a more natural state. At right is the Smuggler's Face rock visage in the high-rising cliffs on the Mansfield side of the Notch.

Courtesy — Mrs. Blanche Sanborn
© Harry Richardson — Used by permission

Stowe News Bureau — Mt. Mansfield Co.

Stowe News Bureau — Mt. Mansfield Co.

LANDSLIDE! — Heavy rains in May, 1969 resulted in a landslide which left a great gash in the Mansfield side of Smuggler's Notch (left) and covered Rt. 108 with debris (right).

Craig O. Burt, Jr.

SKI OUTING, 1934 STYLE — Three of the principals in Stowe's early ski development are pictured here during their lunch break on a ski outing which they took about 1934 — from left, Craig O. Burt Sr., Roland Palmedo and Franklin Griffin.

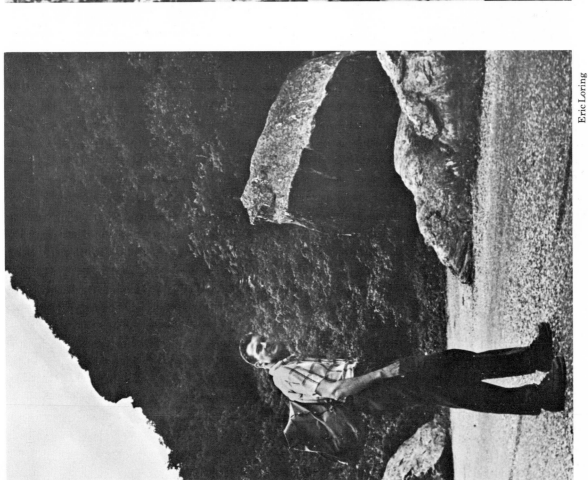

Eric Loring

AUTHOR IN THE NOTCH — The Author, complete with pack for some hiking, poses for the camera in Smuggler's Notch. At right is one of the numerous boulders which have come down over the years from the Notch cliffs; at top left is the notable rock profile of the Hunter and His Dog.

Courtesy — Charles D. Lord
© Harry Richardson — Used by permission

MANSFIELD DEVELOPMENT — A 19th-century book entitled *Picturesque America* carried this illustration (left) of the early Mt. Mansfield Toll Road's Pole Bridge section, a long timber trestle. Above, the famous Summit House as it appeared in the late 1930's or early 1940's; the Chin shows in background. Below is the postmark of the Mount Mansfield Post Office on its last date of issue.

Courtesy — Lester K. Oakes

Courtesy — Stowe Historical Society

TOLL HOUSE, THEN AND NOW — Above is the single Toll House building of the early 1920's. Below is the present Toll House complex with the Toll House Motor Inn at left, the Mt. Mansfield Co. Administration Building at right rear, the Toll House Base Lodge for skiers partly hidden at extreme right (where tolls for the summit road are now collected) and at center the T-Bar skilift engine building.

Photo by the Author

Stowe News Bureau — Mt. Mansfield Co.

AUSTRIAN INSTRUCTOR
MT. MANSFIELD

L. Stearns Gay Jr.

SKIING PRESIDENT — Sepp Ruschp, left, as he appeared in somewhat anonymous fashion in 1936-37, his first season on Mt. Mansfield. Above is Ruschp, since 1953 president and general manager of the Mt. Mansfield Company, Inc., in a photograph taken about 1960. He continues to get out on the slopes nearly every day during the winter season.

ACTION THEN AND NOW — The action was fast at one of Stowe's winter carnivals in the early 1920's (right) when toboggans hurtled down this chute on a slope near the town's public school then known as Simmons Hill. Below is Chuck Ferries in even faster action on Mt. Mansfield's Nose Dive during the downhill race of the 1966 International and U.S. Alpine Championships.

Courtesy — Stowe Historical Society

Stowe News Bureau — Mt. Mansfield Co.

VIEW IN COMFORT — Newest of the Mt. Mansfield Company's lifts is this gondola with enclosed cabins which was completed for the 1968-69 ski season. In the background is the Stowe valley and Worcester Mountains.

Courtesy — Mrs. Jesse Luck

UNDERHILL HALFWAY HOUSE — The first Halfway House on the west side of Mt. Mansfield as it appeared, above, sometime after its construction in 1850. At right is its successor of the 1920's and early 1930's. Sign is a cautionary one to motorists: "Park in Stall."

Courtesy — Mrs. Jesse Luck

42

EASTER PARADE — Mt. Mansfield's annual festive event of 1959 included perennial prizewinner Lewis Bell of Yonkers, N.Y., at left, who won the top award for parade costumes, a season lift pass. Above is the winner of the children's division, Cynthia Eckfeldt, whose title was taken from the then well-known and recently re-established Stowe nightspot. Her prize was the setter dog at right named Mt. Mansfield Nose Dive.

Courtesy — Stowe Historical Society; Stowe News Bureau — Mt. Mansfield Co.

SUNRISE SERVICE — Choir and principals of the Stowe Community Church burst forth in song during one of the Easter Sunrise Services of the 1950's held near the top of the single chairlift on Mt. Mansfield. At right is the Rev. Douglas Brayton, the church's pastor, and at left foreground is Mrs. Brayton, the choir director.

FIRST LADY — Television and newspaper cameras are at the ready as Mrs. Lady Bird Johnson, center, wife of President Lyndon B. Johnson, approaches the double chairlift for a ride to the top of Mt. Mansfield during her visit in Stowe in 1967.

Photo by the Author

MANSFIELD MONUMENTS — Forests and Parks Department Warden Don Bowley, above, views a cairn of rocks on Mansfield's summit ridge known as Frenchman's Pile which marks the site of a man killed by lightning. The author believes, however, the cairn was originally established as a monument to President Ulysses S. Grant. Below, WCAX-Television transmitter crewman Edward Salvas and his son, Wayne, view a monument on Mansfield dedicated in January, 1956 to kick off the annual March of Dimes nationwide fund-raising campaign to fight infantile paralysis. Stones in the base each come from the different state identified. The monument never was completed and is now in some disrepair as well.

Photo by the Author

Stowe News Bureau — Mt. Mansfield Co.

MOUNTAIN TRAGEDY — A Vermont State Policeman views the wreckage of a small airplane which crashed into the upper ridge of Mt. Mansfield on October 6, 1966, killing its three occupants.

CHAPTER
7

Smuggler's Notch

Now why, by the smoke in Smuggler's Notch
My signal fire in the valley,
And your surly sentry, standing watch
Should I knock one whit from the tally?

Last night I drew a picket's fire,
And a Revenue bullet burned me;
Tonight I claim a renegade's hire
And the gold my smuggling has earned me. . . .

You barter your life for glory and fame,
While I run my contraband cattle,
And I'll take my traitor's wage of shame
Though the Devil wins the battle!

WITH THESE MELODRAMATIC STANZAS from a poem by Vermont ballad-writer Morris R. Wilcox* do we introduce the tale which gives name to this dramatic cut between Mansfield and Sterling Mountains. That it is a tale now firmly established as part of Vermont history there is no doubt. But how much it is pure legend and how much "true facts" is a little uncertain.

Illicit trade with Canada was indeed a way of life for a number of Vermonters during the War of 1812 and the several years preceding it. Disintegration of American-British relations had led President Thomas Jefferson to push through Congress the Embargo Acts of late 1807 and early 1808 which forbid export trade with Britain. This and other economic sanctions were the touchstone of United States policy until hostilities culminated in the declaration of war with Britain on June 19, 1812.

Loud protests over the embargo were heard from the Green Mountain State and later there was actual defiance of its enforcement, particularly in the Champlain Valley through which considerable trade was by this time moving to and from Montreal. Initially the embargo applied only to goods moved by ships and vessels but later the ban was extended to all overland movement as well. Vast areas of the state, particularly in its northern reaches, were still largely wilderness and such tracks as crossed these areas provided relatively secure avenues for the movement of smugglers and their goods. That there was such a track

*Wilcox, "The Revenue Runner (War of 1812)," from *Men and Mountains*, Copyright 1959, Golden Quill Press, Francestown, N.H. Used by permission.

through our Notch at this time seems definite. That it was used for smuggling is, however, less certain.

Indians are said to have had a trail through the Notch that was part of a route between Lake Champlain and the Connecticut River Valley. When white men moved into the area trees and bushes were cut sufficient to provide for the passage of pack-horses. A short way through the Notch on the Cambridge side, the path branched, one trail going towards what is now Jeffersonville and the other skirting the west flank of the Sterling Range to Daniel's Notch and then through that and down to Johnson village and roads leading to the north.

The Notch itself is said to have been an exchange point for the illicit goods. By one account, "Smugglers brought silks and drugs from Montreal and hid them in the caves in the Notch, and men from [the Stowe] side took them and sold them in the more thickly settled parts of Vermont, New Hampshire and Connecticut." No mention is made here of cattle moving northward to the British forces but one local and one Vermont historian have each reported that the Notch was a favorite pass by which cattle were smuggled into Canada.

One interesting conjecture on the whole question was provided by E.P. Mudgett of Cambridge in a letter to the *Lamoille Newsdealer* of November 2, 1869. Noting first that "there is some question in this vicinity" about the application of the name, Smuggler's Notch, to the Cambridge-Stowe pass, Mudgett states: "There is no doubt that the route from Bakersfield to Waterville [through what is known as Bakersfield Notch] was a thoroughfare for smugglers and their *attendants*, driving a smart business some fifty years ago — and the reputation of the latter route, may have been charged to the [Cambridge-Stowe] Notch."

Walter J. Bigelow in his 1934 history of Stowe makes an outright challenge of the authenticity of the name: "This must be a piece of imaginative fiction because no evidence of occupation of these dark caverns by anyone has ever been found. Nor is there any indication the Canadians knew the location of this hidden retreat..."

But it takes only one seed of fact which when nourished in the rich soil of human imagination sprouts and grows into a full-leafed legend. Such may be the case with Samuel Slayton Luce's poem, "A Legend Of Smuggler's Notch," the story of which may have been drawn from a mysterious stranger who lived at the Stowe end of the Notch in the years not long before the 1850's when the poem was written. The suggestion of this is that the Notch was not a route for smuggling itself, nor a hiding place for contraband goods, but a retreat for Lake Champlain smugglers when customs officials had got on their trail. The verse chronicle, with some 240 lines, is much too long to reprint here but another writer, Louis J. Paris, has provided a delightful synopsis:

> The story is, briefly, that a band of smugglers has a brush with the customs officers [on Lake Champlain], and in the fight the son of the chief, a lad of twelve years, is knocked overboard and is supposedly drowned. The father, horror-struck at this result of his unlawful pursuit, flies with his wife and daughter to a cabin in Smuggler's Notch, and spends his days in a fine Byronic brand of remorse which has since become obsolete.

> The son was saved by a passing boat. On board are a family of wealth who are going west to settle. They become interested, take him with them and finally adopt him. He grows to manhood and achieves wealth but cannot conquer a yearning to see his parents. He arrives in Burlington, recognizes one of the old gang, learns where his people are hiding and forthwith starts across Mt. Mansfield to join them.

> In the cabin, the father is having his usual remorse, but stimulated by a coming

thunder storm, goes "on high" and reveals the cause of his remorse. A terrific storm breaks with frightful thunder and lightning. In a lull, calls for help are heard from the cliff above. They turn out with lights and rescue a handsome young stranger who has all but been carried over the cliff on a landslide. They take him to their cabin, restore him and he tells the story of his life. Recognition follows and the story ends by the son taking his people back to the happy west with him. Long lost sons have come home in many ways, but this long lost son who comes home riding an avalanche from the Chin down Hell Brook, to an accompaniment of tornado, thunder and lightning, exhausts the dramatic possibilities of the situation, and has all other long lost sons of record beaten to a frazzle.

Another story, equally melodramatic if that's possible, is *Smuggler's Notch — A Tale of the Green Mountains* written by Frank H. Craig, probably some time in the 1920's or 1930's. This has to do with young Henry Matthews of Burlington who upon his appointment in 1808 as chief of the U.S. Revenue Service for northern Vermont pledges to get one Sandy McPherson, leader of a notorious band of smugglers. After various plot intricacies the showdown comes at a cave hide-out in the Notch where McPherson and some of his followers have holed up after being chased there by Matthews. After one inconclusive skirmish and a two-days siege the brave revenue officer sneaks up and plants a keg of powder inside the cave. When this explodes a "great landslide" buries the cave and its evil-doers inside. But all evidence of these dramatic happenings is not lost: a spring which was inside the smugglers' cave escapes the landslide and this is — you guessed it — the Big Spring which gushes from the Sterling side of the Notch.

So those are the facts, such as they are, and the legends which gave Smuggler's Notch its name. It might be added here that the Vermont Board of Historic Sites gives the early 19th century smuggling through the Notch official standing with an historic sites marker located there. Adding to the tradition are tales, none confirmed by this writer, that the Notch was used for smuggling alcoholic beverages from Canada in Prohibition days.

Smuggler's Notch originally lay within the town of Sterling but this town, like Mansfield, has passed into history. Sterling, which was chartered in 1782, had a problem similar to Mansfield's: it straddled two ranges of mountains which made communication difficult among residents of the several areas where settlement had taken place. In 1855 the remainder of the town was divided and different portions annexed to Stowe, Morristown and Johnson. The Cambridge-Stowe line is located well down the southerly side of the Notch proper, a point of some significance which will be returned to in Chapter 11.

As Capt. Alden Partridge described it in the account of his climb of Mt. Mansfield in 1818, the Notch was "a narrow passage through the mountain, which nature appears to have designed for a road." In fact, by that year a company had already been formed to build what was to be known as the Mansfield Turnpike. This private road was never built, however, and it was not until the late 1860's that the towns of Stowe and Cambridge joined forces to open something of a road all the way through the Notch. This fell into disrepair and subsequently was declared unsafe for travel but the two towns later appropriated funds for an improved road suitable for carriages which was completed in 1894.

It wasn't long before outright dissatisfaction was being expressed over this public way. A later Cambridge chronicler was to report that the road "was a joke to say the least." The town's voters, it seems, had understood the road was to be an easy, even grade, "Instead," according to this source, "the contractor followed the old bridle path almost in toto with the result that there were three hills so steep they were not practical for use except by light rigs..."

One of those hills, the last and longest and steepest before the Notch proper, became known as Dead Horse Hill after the horses which foundered in their efforts to make the grade. One such incident is cloaked in a bit of mystery. In August, 1895 a traveler through the Notch came across a horse and carriage which had gone off the road at the bottom of the steep hill in question. The horse was dead in its harness and the carriage turned over and badly damaged but the owner was nowhere to be found. One news account of the incident concluded in appropriately ominous tones: "The horse lies dead, in this lonely spot, the broken carriage and other effects have been taken in charge by the Cambridge officers, but the man, Oh, where is he? And the echo from the depths of the lonely caverns doesn't answer."

Some improvements seem later to have been made but it was automobiles, not horses which led to the next major change in the Notch road. With the advent of the horseless carriage Vermont state government had entered the roadbuilding picture and in 1917 the Legislature appropriated $20,000 for a Notch road suitable for auto travel. Work began late that summer but it was not until August, 1921 that the new road officially opened. Automobilists, however, made several unofficial trips through the Notch before that time including one especially noteworthy. Of this the *Morrisville Messenger* of August 20, 1919 provided the following report from Jeffersonville:

> A most unheard of happening occurred on [August 13], when two auto parties with Ford cars from Massachusetts, while enroute for Waterbury via Stowe, took the wrong road, entering Smugglers Notch. They made the trip over the Cambridge side [and] not even a team had thought of making this trip for years. Both parties came out all right but the cars were somewhat demolished.

In 1935 the road through the Notch between Stowe and Jeffersonville and on to the north became state Route 108. By this time hard-surfacing of roads in Vermont had begun but it was not until 1963 that a remaining 1.4-mile "gravel gap" in the Notch was spread with asphalt.

Cars have never driven through the Notch in wintertime as the stretch of road to this day is not plowed. The Vermont Department of Highways has taken and still takes the position that it would be difficult, if not impossible, to get plowing equipment up the 15 per cent grade approaches to the Notch and even if this could be done the road width leaves little room to put the plowed snow. In addition the considerable snowfall would require very frequent clearing — a highly expensive proposition. Even then, the department believes, the road's sharp curves and steep grades would remain very hazardous to negotiate.

But some have viewed winter passage of the Notch as a way of stimulating the area's ski business by providing easier access to and between the Mt. Mansfield and Madonna Mountain ski areas. Recognizing that construction of a year-round road could do major damage to the scenic Notch area, a new and dramatic proposal emerged in recent years as a way to provide that access — a tunnel *under* the Notch. Generally speaking, forces on the Cambridge side have favored the proposal while those on the Stowe side have opposed it. An informal opinion provided this writer by the Highway Department is, however, that the cost of such project would be prohibitive. Thus while the tunnel idea continues to surface in public print from time to time it seems unlikely that it will ever be carried out.

The idea of a tunnel under the Notch is certainly a dramatic one. But it is not the first out-of-the-ordinary transportation proposal for this mountain gap. Back in 1870 W.H.H. Bingham, a prominent Stowe lawyer and entrepreneur, served notice that he would seek a charter from the Legislature for a railroad to run "if deemed expedient, through what is called the Smugglers' Notch between Stowe and Cambridge." But this proposal seems never to have gotten out of the statehouse, much less the roundhouse.

Bingham, however, already had what might have served as a welcoming center for rail passengers should they debark from a train at the Smuggler's Notch depot. In 1862 he had had built a small hotel near the Big Spring which subsequently was known as the Notch House. This apparently was successfully operated for a few years but by 1869 it is said to have been abandoned.

In 1865 stock was being sold in a company which planned to erect another hotel, to be known as the Rural House, directly opposite the entrance to the Notch on the Stowe side. According to a local news account, this was to be "a magnificent structure, costing $100,000 . . . [with] a chapel, school-room, gymnasium, play-grounds, gardens, walks, &c., connected with it, and is to be operated strictly on temperance principles." Prospective investors, however, apparently were overly temperate in providing funds for the enterprise for the Rural House never came to pass. Another 19th century hotel was in fact built on practically the same site as the Notch House but it, too, was an ill-fated venture, closing after only one season's operation about 1896.

Auto travel through the Notch quickly brought new commercial development — and with it concern over what that development was doing to this dramatic wilderness retreat. Not long after the road's opening in 1921 a souvenir and refreshment stand was opened at the Big Spring by Morton Holly of Jeffersonville. And in 1923 D.C. Hawley established for summertime sightseers a three-times-a-day bus run on Sundays from Jeffersonville to the Notch.

In early 1922 a new corporation known as the Smugglers' Notch Spring Co. was formed by four Stowe men and one Morrisville man. Among the variety of resort-type enterprises which the company planned to carry out was the purchase of springs and the bottling of spring water. The writer has been unable to determine if any of the Big Spring water in fact ever became a commercial product. But the company (which was dissolved in 1934) seems to have been responsible for applying the hand of man to the spring in long-lasting form. About 1924 it was dug out and concrete walls poured to create a pool from which the water emerged through several pipes. Around it cobble stones were laid up with cement to form a sort of terrace-retaining wall above and below.

In 1930 or 1931 the site of the early Notch House once again was the scene of building activity. Constructed was what became known as Boulder Cabin though the name was drawn from the numerous Notch boulders around the building, not from its mode of construction. It was basically a souvenir shop and cafeteria-style restaurant but also had accommodations for overnight guests. The establishment was operated by Mrs. L.M. (Pearl) Shafer, a daughter of L.S. Morse of Cambridge who owned vast acreage along the Sterling Range, including the Big Spring area of the Notch. One feature of the place was a trout pool where guests could catch their own fish and have it cooked for dinner.

The life of Boulder Cabin, like its predecessors, was not a long one. In 1940 the state added some 6,000 acres along the Sterling Range, including the cabin area, to the Mt. Mansfield State Forest. With news of the acquisition came word from State Forester Perry H. Merrill that "At the Big Spring where commercial development has caused criticism from out-of-state tourists, it is planned to restore the natural setting. All buildings will be torn down in the Notch and any other artificial development will be removed." That was done and today one is hard-pressed to find any evidence of that one-time development. The exception is the spring itself where some of the cement and rock walls still remain but nature continues its slow recovery here.

Today there is a parking lot just over the height of land on the Cambridge side. Here are toilet facilities and a small stone shelter where Forests and Parks Department employe Leon Safford dispenses information about the Notch along with literature on other local attractions and events. There are several other small pull-off areas near the Big Spring and elsewhere but that is all. About a mile and a half down the road towards Stowe is a large picnic area with stone fireplaces and tables.

Before leaving the subject of man's structures in the Notch notice must be taken of one other establishment. This is Barnes Camp which is actually two miles down the Stowe side but throughout its existence has had a close spiritual as well as geographical association with Smuggler's Notch.

To carry out a major logging job in the Sterling Mountain area, Willis M. Barnes, prominent Stowe lumberman, built a two-story frame camp in 1910 or 1911 for his winter-time work crews. The start of the Long Trail in the Mansfield region by the Green Mountain Club about this same time stimulated a flow of hikers and other visitors to the area and Barnes was soon providing summertime accommodations for these at the camp.

In 1915, however, he shifted his logging operations further along the Sterling Range and built a new camp in that area with the result that Barnes Camp, as it now was known, was to be closed for visitors. But an arrangement was made with the Green Mountain Club for its opening with three University of Vermont students in charge of the place. Then during World War I the camp was closed except for use by one of the crews working on the Notch road improvements at this time. It re-opened in 1919 with several UVM students again in charge for the GMC and seems to have continued on that basis for several more years though the record is uncertain.

The year 1927 brought a major physical change in the camp but not in its purpose as a base camp for hikers. The C.E. and F.O. Burt Co., which now owned the property, tore down the old camp and built a new, but still rustic, structure of logs and rough lumber. Among its features was a big fieldstone fireplace taking four-foot logs. There were private rooms for 16 guests and a bunkroom for about 30 more. The place was leased for a five-year term to Miss Gladys Bryant.

In 1932 four men took over Barnes Camp with one of them, Chelsea F. Lyons, becoming sole owner a short time later. This was also the year of first stirrings of ski development on Mt. Mansfield and Lyons was soon operating winter as well as summer. He is credited as the first to issue regular snow reports for the mountain, sending these out weekly on penny postcards to his guest mailing list.

Lyons enlarged the main camp building and added several cabins across the road. Using his engineering background, he also installed an ingenious electric system by building a dam on the Notch Brook behind the camp from which a sluiceway fed water to a water-wheel generator which he also built himself. Several years ago Lyons began billing his place as Lyons Lodge — Nearest All Ski Lifts; he continues to take winter guests on a limited basis.

Note was made in Chapter 4 of geologists' thinking on how the forces of nature created the Notch. Whatever the cause, the result is one of the Green Mountains' more unusual gaps — unusual because it runs north and south in line with the main mountain range rather than across it as do other of Vermont's better-known notches.

The floor of Smuggler's Notch stands at 2,162 feet of altitude and above it rise the sheer cliffs of the Mansfield and Sterling massifs a thousand feet or more. On the east, or Sterling, side is one distinctive buttress known as Elephant's Head. The top of the head is the top of the cliff and the lower part narrows to form the trunk. Unfortunately, that elephantine schnozzola has lost some of its original majestic form. In the spring of 1964 the *Stowe Reporter* carried a story under the headline, "The Elephant's Trunk Shrunk;" this told of a group of local residents who had discovered that a major portion of the trunk had departed the head, leaving a 30-foot swath through the trees down to the floor of the Notch.

The Notch cliffs in another way provide one of nature's more striking displays of beauty and grandeur. With the spring run-off of snow-melt and sometimes with heavy rains, a number of waterfalls, some lace-like, a few larger torrents, descend the cliffs into the chasm below. Of particular note in this regard is the cliff face on Mansfield northerly of the Notch proper.

Rising from the Notch floor on both sides are great piles of rock debris loosened from the cliffs above by flowing water and freezing and thawing ice. Within the jumble caves have inevitably formed, the most notable of which is Smuggler's Cave. Located near the state information booth, this is a great pile of boulders surmounted by another huge chunk of rock forming a large chamber which could hold 50 people by one estimate. The cave does have a wide main entrance to its interior but for those of an adventurous sort it is said that one can leave by an underground crevice and re-emerge in daylight a hundred feet away (the writer as a non-speleologist has not confirmed this). And in days of mid-summer heat, air at a cool 49 degrees issues from a gap between several large rocks nearer the road; this is billed as the Natural Refrigerator.

Some of the larger boulders spaced out in the middle of the Notch floor have their own individual stories. Except for one case, however, determining which of the numerous boulders are those referred to is, unfortunately, difficult. But their stories at least can be told.

The earliest named of these is Barton's Rock (or Burton's or Berton's or Burden's Rock as it has variously been known or spelled). This is said to be near the height of land on the Cambridge side and is probably the huge boulder on the Mansfield side of the road about 100 yards above the state information booth though this is right *at* the height of land.

Of two stories told about the naming of this rock one is the more firmly established and the more likely to have been the case; this holds that the rock came down in 1808 (or 1811 as some sources have it) with a terrific shock that was felt all around the area. On that very day a child was born to a family named Ingraham who lived near the Notch in what was then the town of Sterling but later became Cambridge. The new son was called Barton (or Berton) and as one chronicler has put it, "Whether [the birth came] as a direct result of the concussion or [was] mere coincidence, history is silent, but in that family the boulder was ever afterward called 'Barton's Rock'."

The second tale begins in 1873 when a group of visitors were taken in a carriage to the Notch by a local resident. As they passed this rock they saw a haggard old woman gazing intently at it but when they hailed her to inquire if there was some difficulty, "she turned about fiercely and shaking her fist, hustled down a bypath out of sight." The carriage driver then tells all as follows:

> [T]he story is that this hag, which you see, came up here thirty years ago with a party of gay friends, on a rough and tumble climb of Mount Mansfield. The party camped out on the top of the mountain. One day a young fellow, named Berton, of the party, went off for a stroll, and was seen in the ravine waving his hat. This hag, then a young lady, and engaged to Berton, of course, wanted a good sight of her lover. So she crept to the very edge of a shelving rock and leaned over to salute him. Immediately the rock began to loosen, and the young lady had just time to get off, when it fell. Of course it fell on Berton, and there he lays now under that stone; and to cut the story short, this old woman comes here every summer, and we often see her as you see her just now....

Our scene now shifts to four boulders in the Big Spring area and its site for the several hostelries beginning with W.H.H. Bingham's Notch House. In the late 1850's or 1860 a geologist named Albert D. Hager was investigating the Notch and christened a boulder

130 feet north of the spring as Bingham's Rock after the erstwhile Stowe lawyer. Hager described this stone as 35 feet long, 25 feet high and 21 feet wide. It had several large trees growing out of it, hence was a rock which had come down some years before. Another rock described as over 80 feet in length, 25 feet high and 30 feet wide and also with large trees growing out of it was named by Hager as C. Allen Browne's Rock "in allusion to the jovial and gentlemanly companion who accompanied us to the spot." The location given for this is less precise, only further north of the spring beyond Bingham's Rock. The writer feels he did locate these two boulders with Bingham's Rock sitting on a shelf above and behind the spring a short ways and C. Allen Browne's Rock a huge elongated stone just north of the spring and right next to the road.

In October, 1868 Bingham himself and E.B. Sawyer, editor of the *Lamoille Newsdealer*, discovered two large rocks which had come to rest about 165 feet from the Notch House in a recent avalanche. Sawyer described them this way: "One stands upright like a tower. The other presents a flat upper surface, large enough for a dancing hall — being about 30 feet by 16, and quite smooth. In this rock we found plenty of crystallized quartz, one piece of which reflected most beautifully the solar rays, and brother Bingham and ourself christened it 'Prism Rock'." A later chronicler seems to have got the sound of the name somewhat altered, ending up with the interesting result, Prison Rock.

The fall of one of the largest boulders in the Notch occurred on a December night of 1909 shortly before Christmas. Only this one, subsequently christened King Rock and located just below the height of land on the Stowe side, carries an identifying marker. This is a bronze tablet which was set into the rock with appropriate ceremonies in 1941 by Mrs. C.F. Eddy and the Stowe Woman's Club. This gives the time of the rock's fall as the spring of 1910.

Another natural feature of the Notch, the Big Spring, has been mentioned several times already but more details are in order here. Local residents seem to have toned down their estimate of its size for in the 1800's and early 1900's it was generally referred to as the Mammoth Spring. In any event, the spring's large flow emerges out of nowhere from the base of Sterling Mountain to form its own brook which joins the main Notch Brook a short ways down towards Stowe. A number of accounts have ascribed to the spring both an unchanging volume of flow and an unchanging temperature — but each account differs in the particulars. The volume of flow in fact changes considerably. With post-winter run-off the whole hillside around the spring is spouting little gushers; the flow then subsides with the summer season. The writer did not check the temperature at different times but it probably ranges around 40 degrees.

The source of all the water is of some interest. During the 19th century and well into the 20th geologists considered the spring to be an outlet for Sterling Pond which lies some 2,000 feet above in a little bowl formed by the summits of Spruce Peak and Sterling Mountain. Robert A. Christman in a recent geological report had this to say, however:

> The source of the [Big Spring] is not known although it is likely that, like most springs, it is derived from an underground drainage system [within Spruce Peak]. . . . The belief that the spring is related to Sterling Pond is unfounded. It is unlikely that surplus water could be drained from Sterling Pond because it already maintains a delicate balance between the supply of water from rain and snow [on its small watershed] and the output of water to the stream flowing to the north.

Christman's mention of Sterling Pond's outlet to the *north* is also of some interest. This outlet is in fact an artificial one which reverses the original natural flow from the pond to the south towards Stowe. The story is that back about 1865 the operators of a sawmill down the Cambridge side needed an additional source of water for what was then a water-powered mill. Using dynamite they blasted out the new northerly outlet, dropping the level of the pond about ten feet and leaving the Stowe outlet high and dry.

And so we return to our point of departure, the cliffs which rise so dramatically above the Notch floor. Note has been made of Elephant's Head, a rock configuration in which the human imagination has found an image. This is only the beginning of the Notch's picture gallery.

Among the best known of other profiles and figures are the Hunter and His Dog on the Sterling side, and the Singing Bird and Smuggler's Face on the Mansfield side. A visitor in 1924 appears to refer to this last as well as two other profiles in a somewhat wry account: "For the first time . . . we saw the man's face, and the bear guarding the entrance to the Notch — but we couldn't find the woman. Either she had taken to the woods or was only seen in [pre-Prohibition] days, when the imagination was a little keener than it is today."

But the champion picture-spotter seems to have been a Cambridge resident and colorful character named Fred M. LeBaron who established himself as a guide in the Notch in the later 1920's. A local news account tells of his having found some 20 new figures in the cliffs including: ". . . the watch dog, the British soldier of the time of the Revolution, the Kaiser, a pony's head, a monkey, the Man in the Moon, a Dutch Cleanser woman, an old man crying, a woman's face, the profile on Burton rock, a small dog, a turtle, a lion's head, a rabbit, and so on."

For the last ten years or so the Notch has had another character of sorts. He is John Wagner, now 77, who bills himself as the "Whittler Wonder of the U.S.A." He does indeed whittle. Some of his more extraordinary works are interlocking figures-of-eight, balls inside of cubes and intricate winding "ropes," each continuous and each cut from a single piece of wood. But for summer and fall visitors he mostly carves small bears and squirrels. Wagner appears nearly every day in his small red car (he used to ride a motorcycle) to set out his wares which include, among other things, plywood wall-shelves which he makes at his shop in Johnson. He also plays the banjo and harmonica and can issue such sound effects as a beagle on a rabbit's trail, a rooster crow and the sound of a cat whose tail has just been stepped on.

And on that somewhat noisy note we bring to a close our story of Smuggler's Notch though several footnotes will appear in later chapters. We return now to Mt. Mansfield and man's assorted endeavors — some realized, many not — to get up the mountain, stay on the mountain and get down it again, all with greater interest, ease or comfort.

CHAPTER 8

Summit House Saga

SURVEYOR IRA ALLEN undoubtedly was right when, after clambering over our mountain's slopes, he concluded that the town of Mansfield wasn't worth a plugged nickel because its rugged terrain was so unsuited for agriculture. Remembering that Vermont was once just about *all* wooded wilderness, this remote little patch of mountainous timberland was, in the economic terms of the 1770's, like a pail of sand in the Sahara Desert.

The first job for pioneers in the Mansfield area was to clear those "worthless" acres of woods for crops and livestock. But burning the timber to produce potash or "pearlash" brought some immediate economic return. This was sold for hard-to-come-by hard cash — though in pitifully small amounts for the work involved — and continued to be carried out in the remaining woodlands not cleared for agricultural purposes. Thus while the mountain at this point was still very inaccessible, Mansfield's first contribution to human well-being was perhaps its timber for potash.

Timber for lumber was the mountain's next boost for the local economy (and this continues to some extent to the present time). During the 19th and early 20th centuries a number of sawmills and shops for producing woodenware products operated at Mansfield's base on the Notch and Ranch Brooks which join in front of Heyers' Ski Inn on Rt. 108 to form the West Branch stream.

A key logging area for some years has been the Ranch Valley out of which the Ranch Brook flows. The valley takes its name from one Joe Bashaw who in 1843 built a cabin in this mountain wilderness and set about carving out a living. His isolated "pitch" became known as The Bashaw Ranch which subsequently was shortened to the Ranch or Ranch Valley. Owner of much of this area has been the C.E. and F.O. Burt Co., which logged it extensively, and its corporate successor, Burt Forests, Inc.

Credited as the first to promote Stowe and the mountain as a summer spa was Stillman Churchill. In 1850 he converted his dwelling in Stowe village to a hotel known as the Mansfield House (this is now part of the Green Mountain Inn) and began an advertising campaign to draw patronage to his place "for the purpose of enjoyment and rusticating in one of the pleasantest country villages in the state, and the visiting of OLD MANSFIELD MOUNTAIN . . ."

A few people by this time had climbed the mountain for sheer pleasure and adventure but they did so with only a rough trail or no trail at all, particularly on the Stowe side. It was immediately clear that easier access to Mansfield's summit had to be provided if it was ever to successfully attract city-folks. In 1851 a road was built part way up the mountain's eastern ridge and by 1853 a carriage road had been completed to a large spring about half-way up and a bridle trail cleared to within a half-mile of the Nose.

Credit for the provision of the first "permanent" shelter on Mansfield's summit ridge goes, however, to two Underhill men about which more will be noted in Chapter 11. This was a platform tent set up in 1856 near the base of the Nose. Before Churchill could bring to fruition his own plans in this direction he had fallen into financial difficulties and the holder of a mortgage on his hotel, one William Henry Harrison Bingham, took over the property. It was Bingham, a lawyer and one of Stowe's most prominent figures, who really brought the town into its first golden period of tourism.

Bingham owned vast acreage on Mansfield and he immediately moved ahead on what Churchill had started. In 1856 he built at the large spring already mentioned a small guesthouse which promptly became known as the Halfway House. The following year he built a second hotel far up on the east ridge at a point near the site of the present Octagon. Then in 1858 this house was moved a half-mile to a new site just under the Nose. Thus began what was to be a 100-year career for this interesting hostelry. First known as the Tip Top House, sometimes the Mountain House, and at a later period the Mt. Mansfield House, the Summit House is the name it carried for most of its life and this will be used hence-forward.

The first Summit House building quickly proved to be too small. By the start of the 1860 summer season Bingham had had constructed an addition which became the main facility for guests while the original building became an ell and was converted to a dining room, kitchen and quarters for the help.

The Stowe attorney hardly stood still at this point, however, but moved both to protect the summit establishment and to create what for the town was to be one of its most illustrious guest accommodations. On September 30, 1859 he deeded to the University of Vermont some 400 acres along Mansfield's summit ridge. (John B. Wheeler of Burlington, with whom Bingham in some way jointly owned the property, deeded the same tract to the University in a separate instrument.) Bingham's conveyance was not a gift, however, but cost the University $1,000. It also carried a condition limiting use of the property to "scientific purposes" and except for such purposes barred the cutting or burning of any timber or undergrowth. Bingham's intention, it appears, was to see the mountaintop preserved in essentially its wilderness state.

As for the Summit House, which lay within the bounds of this property, the University granted back to Bingham a perpetual lease ("as long as grass grows and water runs") on some 20 acres across the ridgeline and including the hotel. Yearly rental was to be "One Cent" due January 1 each year.

The Summit House was proving a worthwhile investment but it was in the Stowe valley that Bingham embarked on a much larger venture. In 1859 he secured from the Legislature a charter for the Mount Mansfield Hotel Company and then induced nine investors to join him in putting up $10,000 — a total of $100,000 — for the enterprise. In 1864 the doors opened to the company's huge Mansfield House on Main Street in the center of Stowe village. With later enlargement this accommodated 600 guests. After settling in, many of them would take a side trip for one or more nights to the Summit House whose ownership had now passed to the new company. Initially the "big house" flourished but in later years business fell off. On October 4, 1889 the huge frame building was leveled in what to date has undoubtedly been Stowe's most spectacular fire.

The Summit House again was largely on its own. But in the years before this changes and improvements were being made to the mountain facilities, most notably the upgrading of that portion of the summit road above the Halfway House so that carriages could use it. To carry this out Bingham in 1868 had organized and sold stock in the Mount Mansfield Turnpike Company; construction began shortly thereafter and was completed about 1870.

One of the road's more notable features was a log trestle some 100 yards long that spanned a chasm about three miles up. One can imagine the feelings of carriage passengers as they rattled over the corduroy surface peering into the depths below. This stretch came to be known as Pole Bridge Hill and has another special spot in the history of this road. Tolls charged were collected at the top. Near the Pole Bridge were the remains of a lumber camp and to avoid paying the charge, some people would leave their teams at the camp and walk the final mile or so to the top. When the proprietor learned of the trick the buildings were destroyed.

As for the hotel itself, Bingham in late 1863 or early 1864 again expanded the place and further improvements were made in the early 1890's. In 1897 a telephone line was laid up the mountain to put the Summit House in direct connection with the outside world. Major enlargement and improvement of the facilities was carried out in the 1920's, further details of which will be provided shortly. But at this point one note on the early ownership of the Summit House is of some interest.

Founder W.H.H. Bingham owned the establishment until October 6, 1864 when he conveyed the Summit House complex along with other of his Stowe holdings to the Mount Mansfield Hotel Company for $8,000. By 1870 the hotel company had hit hard times and on March 6 that year its stockholders authorized the sale of the company's holdings, including the big Mansfield House, in order to relieve their debts. Twenty days later all the property was conveyed to four Boston men along with, again, W.H.H. Bingham. The price was $50,000, a considerable drop from the original investment of well over $100,000.

References in these last two conveyances are of interest for their allusion to the Summit House property. Bingham's conveyance to the hotel company clearly identifies the 20 acres of summit land as leased from the University of Vermont. But the hotel company's deed back to the five men makes no reference to the lease and appears to convey actual title to the land. This is of some significance for in all the several later changes in ownership no further reference is made to the Summit House land as leased rather than owned. A spokesman at UVM's Land Records Office told the writer that it was his understanding that the University had converted the lease of the 20-acre parcel to a title at some point but if so no record of this is readily available. So the change from lease to title of the Summit House land remains something of a mystery.

Following 1870, the Summit House and Toll Road passed through several hands until 1905 when it was acquired by Walter M. Adams. On January 9, 1920 Adams conveyed the property to a new Mount Mansfield Hotel Company which in turn subsequently became today's Mt. Mansfield Company, Inc.

Why did people come to the Summit House during this 19th century and early 20th century era and what did they do after they got there? Health was one key promotional element with management of the big Mansfield House and the Summit House billing the area as a haven for "hay fever patients or those threatened by the monster."

As for activities, there was, of course, the mountaintop wilderness to scramble over and valley views to behold. But in addition there was the "tight-ship" atmosphere of the inn itself as noted in a fine capsule description provided by Mattie Whiting Baker in her account of a day's visit in 1866:

> There is a sitting room, bar-room, dining room, kitchen and several bedrooms on the lower floor, and the whole upper story is finished off in cozy bedrooms, making accommodations for 50 people. ... The sitting room was com-

fortably furnished with chairs, lounges, a stove in which a fire is always burning.
A center table, on which lay a Bible and a pack of cards. . . . [After climbing the
Nose, Mrs. Baker and her party returned to the hotel for noon-day dinner.]
The crowd thickened, but though faces were unfamiliar, so unconventional are the
rules of mountain etiquette, that we learned the names of many strangers and
conversed with them on general topics. . . .

But all was not solely congenial conversation and quiet card games at the hotel.
According to an 1862 news account, "The visitors have 'hops' and concerts, nearly
every evening, and enjoy themselves finely." And a croquet court was later provided
by Proprietor Adams. One distinguished guest, the famous American poet and essayist,
Ralph Waldo Emerson, described how in the morning following his overnight stay
"a man went through the house ringing a large bell, and shouting Sunrise." In response
guests rumbled out of their beds to climb the Nose for a pre-breakfast view of the sun's
emergence.

And so we arrive at January, 1920 when the new Mount Mansfield Hotel Company
acquired the property from Walter Adams. The company was formed by a group of
Stowe and Morrisville men and one Burlington man, Max L. Powell, who subsequently
served for a number of years as the corporation's president.

While automobiles had by now traveled to Mansfield's summit ridge, the carriage
road was not really adequate for this purpose. Viewing accessibility for the burgeoning
motor vehicle as essential to success, the company's plans, originally developed by Adams,
included major improvements to the road as well as expansion of the hotel facilities
themselves.

The road work, completed in 1922, included realignment of sharper curves and
overly-steep grades, replacement of some 75 waterbars with steel culverts, the elimination
of the famous Pole Bridge, and an overall even gravelling with rock crushed on the site.
In charge of the work was Craig Burt Sr. The project was, in the words of one newspaper
editor, the "most stupendous job of road-building we have ever seen in Vermont."

As for the hotel, it ended up with some 50 rooms — all with a view, of course — plus
a dining room seating well over 100 guests and transients (the floor of this became
"slightly like a roller coaster") and a garage for guests' automobiles. Various facilities
for the guests' comfort, relaxation and entertainment included a new billiards room and
sun parlor. A big stone fireplace was also built, supplementing an old Round Oak stove
in the lobby, which itself was enlarged for dancing parties. Here also were an upright
piano, Captain's chairs and Boston rockers, and "yellowing photographs on the walls."

Such were the facilities and atmosphere of the Summit House for the remaining
40-odd years of its existence (it was called the Mt. Mansfield House for a time during
this period). Activities remained largely the same, of course, but with some embellish-
ments. C.A. Riley, a long-time manager during these years, reports: "Had great times in the
evening, had a phonograph and records and we danced an hour or so every night on the
porch." And younger guests, Riley indicates, at times had an even more enlightened con-
ception of informality than was the case indicated by Mrs. Baker: "Boys tried to get
into girls' rooms one night — called [their] counselor and had quite a time with those
devils, older boys."

Before turning to the final years of this Mansfield institution, the record would be
totally lacking without some sampling of the more colorful gatherings and incidents
occurring here, and other "fascinating trivia" of the guests, staff and, yes, animals
connected with the hotel.

One notable assemblage, reported to be the "largest party that ever spent a night on the mountain," was a convention of the Vermont Press Association in June, 1921. Eighty-five editors and their wives turned out which, to say the least, strained the 50-guest capacity of the house (this was before the new hotel company's major expansion).

Accommodations in and *around* the hotel were what can only be described as varied. One man slept in an automobile parked in the yard while several took cushions from other autos and slept on the lobby floor. There was "the man who stretched his form on a bench in the ladies' parlor" and others who hiked the two-plus miles to the Green Mountain Club's Taft Lodge "and found good accommodations." Summed up the *Grand Isle Star* of the bunking arrangements: "Everyone had a place even if Editor Belnap had to sleep on a settee six inches wide and 'Harry' Parker on the wood box."

While the Vermont newsmen praised the hotel management for its good service to the large crowd, these guests, like others, were quite accommodating in meeting the exigencies of life on the summit. One other illustration of this occurred on July 22, 1926 when the Summit House was struck by a powerful wind and hail storm. The hailstones, "some as big as baseballs," broke every window on the hotel's west side — 220 panes of glass in all. Even before the storm was over, glass, putty and other repair materials had been ordered by phone from the valley below and arrived by truck a short while later. Guests pitched in and most of the damage was repaired by nightfall.

Buffeting by such weather was, of course, in the natural order of things for the sturdy hotel with its summit exposure. On at least two occasions in earlier years winter winds blew its porch off. Guy wires subsequently anchored both this and the roofs of the several buildings to bedrock.

As for the staff, clerks in the early days were accustomed to adding personal comments to the register. For July 4, 1875 there was this note: "100 years ago the Declaration of Independence was signed. President Grant is much below G. Washington in national affairs." There is also the story told of one Bert Newcity who worked at the hotel. It seems he was a great prankster and on one occasion took a large stuffed bear up on the Nose and in full view of some of the hotel guests caused it to topple off, much to the consternation of all.

As for *real* bears, the hotel company for several years kept a bear mascot though this was housed at the Toll House at the start of the Toll Road rather than at the Summit House. It was domestic animals, however, which added a greater part to the Summit House tradition.

Among these was the line of bovines kept at the hotel to provide guests with fresh dairy products. The first cow of record, though her name is not known, put in what probably was a record 17 years of service on this lofty feeding ground. She was succeeded by Dolly who seems to have developed a considerable attachment to her summer duty; when brought down to the village for the winter, according to one report, "she returned invariably to the summit as often as she could escape." Other cows followed but no complete record of the Mansfield bovine honor roll is available.

A key to the success of the Summit House in pre-carriage road days were the mounts provided for the ascent between the Halfway House site and the hotel. These seem to have been a mixed bag of horses, ponies and donkeys. The descent of Mansfield on horseback was particularly unnerving for most riders. One published set of instructions for the downhill ride may or may not have induced confidence: "Don't guide the horse. Simply hold on. You will feel the strong inclination to go over the horse's head. Just keep in the saddle and let the animal 'slide'."

A rundown on Summit House animals has to include mention of cats, or at least one of them anyway. These were kept on hand to hold the mouse population in bounds. But one cat, Tip by name, was overly discriminating in his taste, much to the joy of the Summit

House mice. In early June, 1921 the Rileys brought Tip to the top to open up for the season. But the cat suddenly disappeared not to show up again until late that fall and then at the Riley's village home. According to a news account of his reappearance, "The cat had been an excellent mouser and it was expected that he would rid the hotel of mice, but apparently because the mountain mice were different from those he had known in the valley he would not touch them."

Most of the other mountain houses in Vermont had closed down by 1900, but Mansfield's Summit House was still going strong, or going anyway, in 1949. That year the hotel company announced plans for a "much larger and more modern hotel to replace the Summit House" but the plan never materialized.

It was simply old age and changing public preference for less isolated valley accommodations that finally brought the end. On July 26, 1958 the Mt. Mansfield Co. held an open house to mark the hotel's 100 years of continuous seasonal operation. It thus began its second century but that same fall the hotel closed its doors forevermore to overnight guests. For several more years, however, the Mt. Mansfield Co. did operate a snack bar in the building for Toll Road drivers and summit hikers.

But by 1964 it was felt the place had become a hazard to summer visitors. Following the first snowfall in October that year the building was razed and then burned. Other mountain hotels had come to a premature death by fire. But for the Summit House on Mt. Mansfield it was a departure in a final blaze of glory.

CHAPTER 9

Later Development

O PERATION OF Mansfield's Summit House, though it is no longer with us now, spanned the eras of both early and later development on Mt. Mansfield. An even more appropriate symbol of the joining of the old with the new is the Toll Road; it still carries automobiles to the top in the summer as it did horse-drawn carriages a hundred years ago and in the wintertime it is one of the complex of ski trails for which the mountain has become so well-known in the modern era. But before getting to the story of skiing, some back-tracking is in order to review other developments on the mountain, both proposed and actual, during the later 19th century and into the 20th.

Entrepreneurs on the west side of Mansfield early on took steps to follow the lead of W.H.H. Bingham. In the 1860's plans were announced for a track to be laid up this side over which an engine at the top would draw a car with a cable. Somewhat later, considerable planning was carried out for a west slope toll road. Neither idea, of which more details will be given in Chapter 11, ever was realized. Interest in a railroad up the mountain crystallized several times around the turn of the century but nothing ever materialized on this idea either.

With the arrival of the automobile the new Mount Mansfield Hotel Company, as we have seen, improved the Toll Road to make it suitable for standard cars — and standard drivers. The company seemed content to rest there. But in 1926 the *Waterbury Record* threw out a proposal for a skyline drive between the Nose and the Chin. The *Barre Times* was strongly opposed to the idea, contending the summit area should be left to hikers. With a road, the *Times* said, "it would be a lazy man's lolling place then."

Nothing happened on this but seven years later a proposal for a scenic highway the length of the Green Mountains descended upon the state in a flurry of controversy. This was resolved only after several years and then with rejection of the idea. Known as the Green Mountain Parkway, the route developed would not have impinged directly on Mt. Mansfield but would have passed through Underhill somewhat to the west. The idea for a Green Mountain highway was revived in 1964 in connection with a federal program of scenic roads and parkways but according to the Vermont Department of Highways the plan for this has assumed a very inactive status.

About the same time that improvements to the Toll Road were making the mountain more accessible for land vehicles, a proposal — or at least a prediction — for a summit landing strip for air vehicles made its appearance. The occasion was the first flight over

Mansfield on September 19, 1920, details of which appear in Chapter 13. A passenger for this historic trip was Cornelius L. McMahon of Stowe. When safely back on the ground at an airstrip just south of Stowe village McMahon predicted "that within a few years a field will be laid out between the Nose and Chin of Mt. Mansfield and planes will be landing there." The idea, it appears, never got off the ground.

Technical developments of a different sort led to the first new construction on the summit ridge beyond the Summit House. In November, 1947 the University of Vermont provided the state's Department of Public Safety with a lease on a 250 by 250 foot piece of land where the department subsequently erected an antenna and building for radio transmission equipment. This small complex lies on the open ridge several hundred yards north of the Summit House site. The antenna tower was the first of what were to become several overgrown whiskers for the mountain man's profile.

On May 1, 1954 a bulldozer chugged up the Toll Road pushing aside the three or four feet of snow that remained along the final mile or so. Thus began construction of transmission facilities for the first commercial television station in Vermont. The Federal Communications Commission first assigned the station's call letters as WMVT and when the station went on the air five months later that was its initial identification. Shortly thereafter call letters for the Burlington-based enterprise became WCAX-TV. The station's mountain facilities include a 30 by 40 foot one-story building below the south rim of the Nose with a tall antenna tower at the top of the Nose.

The next broadcast installation to appear was that of Vermont's Educational Television Network. Construction of this antenna and building, which are also located on the Nose, began in 1966 with the station going on the air in October, 1967.

The most recent such installation is that of the Vermont-New York Television Corp., also of Burlington. Another commercial station, WVNY-TV began operations with its summit antenna and building in August, 1968. This complex is located on property of the Mt. Mansfield Co. in the Summit House site area. On April 1, 1971 the company's television station (it also operates a radio station) ceased operations and the status of its summit facilities at this writing is uncertain.

All these facilities are in the immediate area of the Nose or along the ridge saddle slightly to the north. There is nothing on the Chin. But at one point there almost was. In 1958, the U.S. Air Force announced plans for construction on the Chin of facilities for a Bomarc missile ground-air transmitter. These were to include two antenna and a small building plus a road along the west side of the summit ridge from the end of the Toll Road. The Green Mountain Club mounted strong opposition to the installation. And while University of Vermont trustees had agreed to provide a long-term lease on property for the installation, other University representatives were successful in getting the government to consider an alternative road to the Chin area which would mean less damage to the summit ridge itself. While study of that was still underway the Air Force withdrew its plan completely.

To flip back the calendar pages, up to 1914 all of the land encompassing Mt. Mansfield was in private hands except for the summit ridge strip which W.H.H. Bingham and John B. Wheeler had deeded to the University of Vermont. In that year the Vermont Forest Service purchased 3,155 acres of woodland on the west flank of the mountain. This was the start of the Mt. Mansfield State Forest. In 1915 some 1,845 acres in Stowe were added. This piece, which runs down the east slope of the mountain, encompasses about two-thirds of the present-day ski trail and lift complex and thus proved to be an especially critical chunk of property.

Further acquisitions, including several major ones, have been made since then so that the Mt. Mansfield State Forest now extends into Cambridge, Johnson and Morristown on the north and Bolton and Waterbury on the south. The most recent addition, which occurred in late 1970, brought the total area of the state tract to 27,162 acres. This was the purchase of just under 1,900 acres running south of Nebraska Notch.

The Vermont Forest Service (later the Forests and Parks Department) has not, of course, simply sat on this land. Logging has continued on some of it but under controlled conditions. As for development, the state forest now has three campground-recreation areas. Two of these directly connected with Mt. Mansfield are the Smuggler's Notch Campground on Rt. 108 opposite the entrance to the Mt. Mansfield ski area and the Underhill Campground on the opposite side of the mountain. There is also the Little River Campground at the Waterbury Reservoir. All have shelter lean-tos, tentsites and related facilities with the last-mentioned also offering a swimming and boating area.

A proposed development that resurfaced in conjunction with the Forest Service's first purchases of land in this area was that of a road through Nebraska Notch between Stowe and Underhill. The story of that proposal will be told in Chapter 11.

It was establishment of the now famous Stowe ski area that has been the most significant development on Mt. Mansfield involving the state land. Some details of this will shortly be provided but to set the scene a look at the early days in Stowe of this crazy-wonderful winter sport is in order.

Local history has not recorded precisely when the first ski tracks appeared on a snowy field in the town. But Craig O. Burt Sr. has recorded that:

> Around 1902 to 1905 a few of us took hardwood boards and bent up one end, nailed on a toe strap and thought we were ready to ski. The poles were 1″ x 1″ hardwood and quite long — there were no grooves in our skis so control was at a minimum. Our skiing consisted of straight running down a slope near the present [Stowe public school] . . . . But the spills without the thrills was not really skiing, and all of us lost interest. The infection, however, was there.

Credit for a revival of interest in the sport appears to rest with three Swedish brothers who settled with their families on farms in Stowe in 1912 or 1913. One of them, Eric Svedin, hand-crafted a pair of skis — something he had never done before — and soon had orders for others. The children in the Swedish families seem to have been Stowe's first ski instructors, teaching any who would join them in the rudiments of the sport. But the Swedes moved away in 1919 and at that point it was a case of the "experienced" native boys teaching any newcomers to the town's now blossoming sport.

A meeting of a small group of community-minded citizens in the boiler room of the Akeley Memorial Building in Stowe village provides the historic setting for the town's real beginnings as the "Ski Capital of the East." The date of this has not been recorded but it probably was an evening in late 1920. Five or six men including Burt gathered here to discuss the town's economic depression of the post-World War I period and what might be done to lift the gloom. Out of that and a later meeting came plans to hold a winter carnival on Washington's Birthday, 1921. Burt and another man were given the go-ahead to construct both a ski jump and toboggan slide. These were built on Simmons Hill just above the present Stowe public school athletic field.

Community interest and participation built steadily. When February 22 arrived — a beautiful day — various events had been scheduled by the now official sponsor, the Stowe Ski Club, and a crowd estimated at 1,000 turned out. At Simmons Hill, according to local news accounts, "20 big competitive events" were held including snowshoe and toboggan races, half-mile and 220-yard "ski dashes" and, of course, ski jumping.

For non-competitors a number of colorful events were held on Main Street. There was "snow-bicycling, with a bicycle especially made for this sport" and a "toboggan snake dance" in which a tractor drew along a string of toboggans and their riders. Horace Melendy of Jeffersonville furnished thrills when he was drawn on skis by an automobile at 35 miles an hour. An added attraction indoors was an evening minstrel show put on at the Memorial Building auditorium. It was a sell-out — not only were the gallery and all the aisles filled but seats were even sold on the radiators.

About $1,000 was taken in though most of this went to pay for the ski jump, toboggan slide and other expenses. But all told the success of the event "exceeded the most sanguine expectations of those interested in pulling off this great stunt." It would be a hard act to follow.

But followed it was, at least for two years. For the 1922 Stowe Winter Carnival, a four-day event, the facilities on Simmons Hill — renamed Skiboggan Hill — were improved and expanded to include a skating rink. Attendance for the affair was estimated at 2,500. Added to many of the first year's events were ski-joring with ponies and log-hauling competitions for men and their teams. Refreshments were available at a large igloo-style Ice Palace.

The year 1923 saw a three-day event in early February. The first day included an Outdoor Vaudeville Show "consisting of boxing on snowshoes, tug-of-war on skis, basketball in the snow and a masquerade ball." Whether the last meant *dancing* on skis or snowshoes is not known but it is clear the carnival sponsors were not lacking for imagination. The final day was the biggest when the various competitive events were held. But the feature was Daredevil Dobson of Leominster, Mass. who was tied in a strait jacket to a toboggan and freed himself before reaching the bottom of the 1,000-foot chute.

That was the last of these early Stowe winter carnivals. Just why another was not held is uncertain though the loss of the ski jump tower may well have been a factor; a strong wind blew that down the summer of 1923. The toboggan slide, however, continued to be used several years.

Once again the younger generation came to the forefront. For several years after this Stowe High School and Cambridge High School in Jeffersonville held joint winter meets with the site shifting each year between the two towns.

Such were the pioneering days of skiing in Stowe. It may not need pointing out that up to this time Mt. Mansfield had played almost no part in the growth of the sport. But there was one notable exception.

It was the morning of February 1, 1914 when two men arrived at the start of the Toll Road. One was Charles W. Blood of Boston who was wearing snowshoes. The other was Nathaniel L. Goodrich, librarian at Dartmouth College in Hanover, N.H. He had skis on. The two started up the mountain and without difficulty reached the Summit House. After lunch and a rest they started down. Goodrich has left this somewhat wry account:

> I had a lot of fun during the descent, but my stops — voluntary and otherwise — were very frequent. I reached the foot of the mountain somewhat weary but definitely pleased with myself, at least until Mr. Blood hove in sight within a very few minutes after me. His steady plodding down on snowshoes had brought him to the Toll House almost as rapidly as I had been able to do it.

It was an historic trip, probably the first ski run down Mansfield (though Goodrich never claimed that) and certainly the first ever recorded. While Goodrich skied many other places in succeeding years, it was not until March, 1943 that he again visited Stowe to enjoy the sport. In those 29 years a lot had happened on Mt. Mansfield. But for an account of that we shall turn to a new chapter.

CHAPTER
10

The Mt. Mansfield Company

I T WAS LATE WINTER in 1931. A tall, lean man lay in a hospital bed recuperating from a broken leg. The cause of the injury, a skiing accident, had hardly discouraged him for to pass the time he had been poring over detailed topographic maps looking for a mountain area which would be suitable for extended use by members of the amateur ski club of which he was president. A decisive finger came to rest on Mt. Mansfield.

It was early winter in 1936. A 28-year-old sturdy Austrian immigrant who had already made a name for himself skiing in the grandiose Alps stepped off a steamer at New York City. A short while later he had his first look at Mt. Mansfield and was awestruck; it wasn't how big it was, which for Vermonters at least was considerable, but rather how small.

It was the winter of 1945. A 53-year-old man back for his second season of Mt. Mansfield skiing stood in a long line for the one major lift then going up the mountain. He was not the first to be impatient over the delay but he had the interest and wherewithal to do something about it. A short while later he had offered to put up 51 per cent of what was needed for another lift.

With these vignettes we introduce three of the men who played key roles in the development of Mt. Mansfield as one of the earliest and now one of the largest and finest ski centers in the eastern United States. The first man was Roland Palmedo, a New York City investment banker; the second was Sepp Ruschp, then a ski instructor and now president and general manager of the Mt. Mansfield Company, Inc.; and the third was the late C.V. Starr, developer of a worldwide complex of insurance firms.

Other men, of course, and other factors also helped to bring about this development. There was the foresight of Perry H. Merrill, head of the Vermont Forest Service. There was the local interest of such native Stoweites as Craig O. Burt Sr., whom we have already mentioned several times, and George Gale, Mansfield's first "official" snow-conditions observer. And there was Franklin Griffin, one of the ski area's first entrepreneurs and the first president of the Mt. Mansfield Ski Club.

Other factors were the concentration of property on the Stowe side of the mountain in basically two hands, the Burt Co. with its logging domain and the Mt. Mansfield State Forest public land. There was the state road providing access to the base of the mountain and the private toll road to its top. And finally there was the mountain itself with its favorable topography and its average 150 inches of winter snowfall.

All of these factors along with a lot of money from various sources did not come together in simple fashion. More detailed notice of this will be taken shortly but a look is first in order at the transition between Stowe's pioneer winter carnival days and the first blossoming of skiing as a significant new business for the town.

On March 6, 1932 the Stowe Winter Carnival was revived. For this event new facilities were established on what was then the Quincy Magoon farm, now the site of the Pine Motor Court on Rt. 100 about a mile north of Stowe village. These included a 300-foot-long ski jump, a toboggan chute and even a bobsled run. Ski events were the jumping plus a downhill race. About 300 attended the affair, a significant drop in turn-out from those held ten years earlier. Perhaps for this reason the revived Stowe Ski Club expanded its 1933 carnival with the addition of slalom and cross-country races and at least one special attraction — an exhibition of jumping on *one* ski by W.C. McNamara of Norwich University. The estimated turn-out of 1,000 testified to the increased interest.

These carnivals, like the earlier ones, were again centered in the Stowe valley. But in 1932 things began happening up on the mountain and that year can perhaps best be set as the birth year of the present-day Mt. Mansfield ski complex.

The country's massive economic depression at this time contributed in a very direct way to this early development. One of the federal government's recovery programs was the Civilian Conservation Corps. Through the efforts of State Forester Merrill arrangements were made for the CCC crews to carry out trail-cutting projects. On June 9, 1933 a contingent of men arrived at nearby Waterbury and that year cut the first trail on Mt. Mansfield specifically for skiing (the established Toll Road was, of course, being used for this purpose). This was the Bruce Trail which was named after prominent local lumberman H.M. Bruce. The 4½-mile trail ran from a point on the Toll Road near the present junction of the Nose Dive down to near the Ranch Camp (the trail is still traceable though overgrown). Cutting of additional trails including the famous Nose Dive followed in succeeding years.

On Februrary 11, 1934 Mt. Mansfield was the scene of a "down-the-mountain-run" on the Bruce Trail, the first ski race in its history. Out of 13 competitors, Jack Allen of Burlington was the winner with a time of 10 minutes, 48 seconds; Charles Lord placed second with a run of 11 minutes, 17 seconds and Craig Burt Jr. was third in 12 minutes, 35 seconds. Simple pocket watches were used for timing the race. After being synchronized at the Ranch Camp one remained with a recorder at the finish line while the other went with the starter to the top; he was also a competitor who started himself in what Lord later recalled was "a very informal race."

A major stimulus to the ski activity came from the New York City Amateur Ski Club whose president in the early 30's was Roland Palmedo. This chapter's opening vignette told of Palmedo's pinpointing of Mt. Mansfield as the area which seemed to hold the most promise for ski activity for the club. Over Washington's Birthday, 1932, the winter following his accident, he and one Jose A. Machado Jr. journeyed to Stowe to ski and survey the mountain and to talk with local residents and officials. What had looked good on a map was confirmed and the two men went back to the club with a favorable report.

Other things were happening. The Stowe Ski Club reorganized and formally incorporated on January 16, 1934 as the Mt. Mansfield Ski Club. The club in those early days played a prominent role in local growth of the new winter sport, not just in boosting interest in skiing but in actually providing facilities and related services.

The club's first headquarters was the Ranch Camp. In 1932 Craig Burt Sr. had fixed up the old logging camp into ski accommodations for use by boys in the area. In 1933-34 the MMSC in conjunction with the Burt Co. took over management of the rustic establishment and this was the start of a notable landmark in the history of Mt. Mansfield skiing. Its operation continued through the 1949-50 season.

Up to this point the only way skiers could get up Mansfield, even a short ways, was to walk up. For Ranch Campers one climb a day up the 4 ½ -mile Bruce Trail was considered par for the course. With the opening of the Nose Dive some of the hardier skiers managed three trips a day up that.

Then in the winter of 1934 a Model-T truck engine kicked over downcountry in Woodstock and began moving skiers on a long loop of rope up a pasture hill on the Clinton Gilbert farm. It was the first ski tow in Vermont and the United States. But Mansfield was not far behind this historic first. On February 7, 1937 commercial operation of a rope tow began on the Toll House slopes. The lift had been purchased from Wesley Pope of Jeffersonville and installed by him late in 1936 but poor conditions at the start of the season had prevented its earlier operation. It was no Model-T for Mansfield! This first tow, which was 1,000 feet long, was powered by a 1927 *Cadillac* engine. For 50 cents skiers could ride it all day and for $5 could ride it *all* season. A second rope tow, this one 2,000 feet long, was installed the following winter on a slope above the present State Shelter by Franklin Griffin.

In 1935 the famous Skimeister trains had begun their runs to Waterbury just south of Stowe, bringing hundreds of new enthusiasts up from Boston and New York City for weekend outings. For the three-day Washington's Birthday weekend in 1937 more than 800 passengers came to Stowe in what was subsequently described as "the largest overnight skiing expedition ever to be carried by snow train in the United States." That crowd plus an equal number of overnight guests arriving by car *plus* thousands more transients on Sunday, February 21, made up a crush of people in Stowe of historic proportions. The reason was a last-minute transfer of the Eastern Downhill Championship race from snowless Mount Greylock in northwestern Massachusetts to the Nose Dive on Mt. Mansfield. The day of the race produced a monumental traffic jam on Rt. 108 as an estimated 10,000 spectators in 3,000 cars poured into Stowe.

Another significant development was the Mt. Mansfield Ski Club's hiring of a ski instructor for the 1934-35 season, one Jim Trachier, who in that capacity became another first for the mountain. Trachier was engaged the next year as well but the following season the club hired a new instructor. It was Sepp Ruschp.

Ruschp was born in 1908 and brought up in Linz, Austria near the Austrian ski fields. He took up skiing at an early age but was active in other sports as well including track, rowing, mountain climbing — and flying gliders. In 1926 he completed a course in engineering at the Linz Training School and then continued his education at a night business school, at the same time taking private lessons in English. As a competitive skier he was in his prime between 1930 and 1936, winning the Upper Austrian combined championship several times and various notable cross-country events, both individual and relays.

In 1936 the Austrian Ski Association was getting letters from U.S. ski clubs seeking instructors. Compared to Austria and Europe as a whole, the sport here was in its infancy. Ruschp, who now had his Austrian ski teaching license, recognized the possibilities and when one of those letters came from the Mt. Mansfield Ski Club he decided to give up the ski school and sports shop he was operating by that time and accept the club's offer. He arrived in this country December 10, 1936 and not long after had that first awe-struck look at what compared to his native Alps was a miniscule Mt. Mansfield.

Ruschp's ski school staff that first winter consisted of one person — himself — and for many he was known simply as "the Austrian instructor." By the following season he had an assistant, Edi Euller, and a name for the public, the Sepp Ruschp Ski School. He subsequently expanded his staff further with both other Austrians and top American skiers. One of these latter was Kerr Sparks who first joined him in 1939 and who has headed the ski school since 1948. Today the school's staff numbers about 55 regular members.

By 1944 Ruschp had become a director of the Mount Mansfield Hotel Company which had established his ski school as one of its divisions. But bigger things had already begun to emerge for him.

December 9, 1940 was the first day's operation of a major new facility, a 6,300-foot-long single chairlift up Mt. Mansfield. It was the first of its kind in the state and was billed as the longest and highest such lift in the world. Designed by the American Steel and Wire Co., the lift originally carried about 200 skiers an hour. Over the years its operating speed has been increased somewhat and chairs added to bring the present capacity to about 300 an hour. Also constructed in 1940 at the top of the chairlift was the Octagon warming shelter; this was expanded twice in later years.

Sponsor of the chairlift was a new company, Mt. Mansfield Lift, Inc., whose president, Roland Palmedo, was the key mover of the project. He had gathered together a number of interested investors for the $75,000 needed to build the lift. Among these was Lowell Thomas Sr., the well-known world traveller, author and radio commentator whose periodic broadcasts from Stowe provided major publicity for the area.

The chairlift was just one year old when World War II exploded for the U.S. The war had, of course, major effects for the Mansfield ski area. Most of the young men who were at the heart of the mountain's ski services went off to military service, many of them in mountain troop units. Staff of the Sepp Ruschp Ski School and the newly established Mt. Mansfield Ski Patrol was all but non-existent. The Mt. Mansfield Ski Club suspended all meets and events for the duration and put its membership publication on a reduced schedule. Ruschp himself saw service as a pilot flight instructor for the Army Air Force and following his discharge worked as an expediter for Bell Aircraft in Burlington before returning to Stowe (he and his wife Hermine had become American citizens in 1943).

With the end of the war, summer operation of the chair-lift as a tourist attraction began in 1946. But it was the wintertime where things were booming. At 9:31 a.m. February 14, 1953, Mrs. Pat Sweetser of Cambridge, Mass. found herself the chairlift's one millionth rider and for the honor received a gold-plated lifetime pass for all of the area's lift facilities. News reports of the time described the event as the end of an era which proved that the chairlift gamble had paid off.

The *first* official rider on the chairlift that December day in 1940 had been Mrs. J. Negley Cooke Jr., wife of the vice president of the Mt. Mansfield Lift Co. Mrs. Cooke went under the sobriquet of "Nose-Dive Annie" because she "practically lived " on what had become the mountain's most popular trail for advanced skiers. The scope of this work permits only brief mention of some of Mansfield's individual ski trails but the Nose Dive is deserving of special consideration.

The first of a still-growing list of sanctioned competitive events on this trail occurred February 23, 1936. Robert Bourdon, then of Woodstock and later a prominent Stowe skier, writer, photographer and craftsman, became state downhill champion by running the Nose Dive's 1¾ miles in 2 minutes, 35 seconds. In another Nose Dive race, the Men's National Downhills in March, 1938, Sepp Ruschp was the event's only casualty, receiving a dislocated ankle in a bad fall — he was up immediately, however, and still finished 14th.

Abner W. Coleman and Charles D. Lord laid out the trail's original route, an alignment that was basically maintained for many years. Coleman became a traffic engineer for the Vermont Highway Department and was long a director of the Mt. Mansfield Ski Club and for many years editor of its publication, *Mt. Mansfield Skiing*. Lord, a civil engineer and another avid skier, can be said to be the architect of the early Mansfield trail system. The layout of the Nose Dive in 1933 came when he was connected with the local CCC unit which rough-cleared the trail the summer of 1934 and finished the job the following year. In 1940 Lord became manager of the chairlift for the Mt. Mansfield Lift Co. and has been with its successor, the Mt. Mansfield Co., Inc., in various capacities ever since (the Lord Trail has Charlie as its namesake).

The Nose Dive has undergone several major changes over the years. One significant one was its extension in 1952 to the top of the Nose to give an additional 500 feet vertical drop for a present total of just over 2,500 feet. Another change, completed in 1965 for the U.S. Alpine Championships of 1966, was revision of the famous Seven Turns to three wide S-turns.

One bit of tradition for the trail had its origins in the 1930's when a *Nose Dive* ski appeared on the market. One of a line known as *Ski Sport* skis, it was manufactured by the Derby & Ball Co. of Waterbury, Vt. The firm's president later reported that as the *Nose Dive* skis "became distributed more widely throughout the country there were a few who chose to object to the suggestion contained in such a name for a ski." The short-lived honorarium for the Mansfield trail was dropped as a result.

For the 1943-44 season the Nose Dive was still in its pristine form and the chairlift was, besides shank's mare, the only way to get to the top of the mountain. Among those able to get in some Mansfield skiing in this mid-war year were Cornelius Vander Starr and his wife Mary.

Starr's start on a remarkable career in the American tradition began in 1919 when, after Army service in World War I, he became bored with a routine job with a steamship company. Then 27, he used a $10,000 nest egg to establish an insurance agency in Shanghai, China. From that Starr built up a world-wide complex of insurance firms and with it amassed a fortune. His first brush with skiing — at the age of 47 — came at Sun Valley, Idaho in 1940. He took to the sport with avidity, both for its pleasure and for what he saw as a new business opportunity. After his introduction to Stowe and Mansfield in 1943-44 he returned for the greater part of the 1944-45 season. It was at this time that the chapter's opening vignette occurred and he pledged to Sepp Ruschp to put up 51 per cent of the funds needed for another lift. With that began C.V. Starr's key role, both financially and administratively, in the modern era of ski development on Mt. Mansfield. It was to end only with his death in 1968.

The new lift for which Starr (and other) money became available was a T-Bar installed in 1946. Originally about 3,000 feet long it was extended 1,000 feet in 1947 to the top of what became the Tyro, Standard, Gulch and North Slope Trails. For the construction and operation of this a new company had been formed, Smugglers' Notch Lift, Inc.

At this point the different interests on the mountain represented, as one writer has put it, "a mild case of business anarchy." The chairlift was owned by one corporation, the T-Bar by another, the Lodge at Smugglers' Notch (of which more shortly) by a third, and the Summit House-Toll Road-Toll House complex by a fourth, the Mount Mansfield Hotel Company. While Ruschp's ski school was part of the hotel company, the Mt. Mansfield Ski Club, as a fifth interest, was still sponsoring the Mt. Mansfield Ski Patrol which now had paid patrolmen.

The MMSC today is the amateur ski organization which serves as official sponsor for sanctioned competitive events. It holds a number of other races and also sponsors various social and fund-raising events and charter air excursions to foreign ski areas. And finally it maintains a highly-regarded junior ski program. But in its early years the club also played a significant role in the actual development of the Mansfield ski area. A club historian has recorded that not until the present-day Mt. Mansfield Co. was formed "was there any centralized responsibility for ski facilities in the region. The club . . . had acted from the beginning as a general planning and coordinating agency." But that "centralized responsibility" was on its way and Ruschp and Starr have been credited with the principal roles in its eventual establishment.

In 1949 the hotel company acquired 90 per cent of the stock of the Mt. Mansfield Lift, Inc. as the first move in the ultimate total absorption of the latter. The T-Bar on Mansfield was acquired from the Smugglers' Notch Lift Co. that same year and the Lodge at Smugglers' Notch in November, 1950. The final step came in 1951 when the hotel company was renamed the Mt. Mansfield Company, Inc. and re-organized with Starr as president.

In January, 1953 Starr stepped down as president (though remaining as a director and chairman of the board) and personally nominated Ruschp who was elected his successor. In 1961 Starr resigned from the board of directors with Gordon Tweedy succeeding him as chairman. A local news account said the move was in line with Starr's belief that management should be left "in young and vigorous hands" (he was now 69). But his association with the area continued to the end — just a short while before his death on December 20, 1968 he was involved in the purchase of Stowehof, a prominent lodge which subsequently came under Mt. Mansfield Co. management.

Considerable further development of facilities on Mt. Mansfield has occurred since the new company was established. Among the more significant was installation of a Riblet double chairlift parallelling the original single chair. This was dedicated in December, 1960 with Governor, Congressman-Elect and Skier Robert T. Stafford among the notables in attendance (Ruschp was introduced as "the first Austrian to become a native Vermonter in one generation").

In 1967 stockholders approved plans for a major expansion program including snow-making equipment for the Spruce Peak area and a new gondola lift with four-passenger enclosed cabins up to near the base of the Lower Lip. The snow-makers were ready for the 1967-68 season and the gondola for the 1968-69 season together with its Base Terminal, Cliff House and associated complex of five new trails. A tragic accident involving four passengers (all of them injured, two seriously) marred the early operation of this lift when on December 31, 1968 a car became disengaged from the cable, slid back, crashed into a second car and then fell some 25 feet to the ground. The situation was corrected and operation resumed a few days later with approval of the Vermont Tramway Board which inspects and licenses all ski-lifts in the state. No further mishaps have occurred with the gondola since that time. And overall, it might be noted, the Mt. Mansfield Co. has maintained an excellent safety record for its various uphill facilities.

The Little Spruce and Spruce Peak areas have not been mentioned heretofore. In the fall of 1946 the Mount Mansfield Hotel Company had acquired some 3,000 acres in this area and for the 1949-50 season the Little Spruce slopes — or Sunny Spruce Slopes as they were first promoted — had been cleared and were serviced by two rope tows in tandem. (This season had an early opener, November 26, 1949; on hearing the news one man immediately took a taxi from Stamford, Conn.!) For the next season the present 2,000-foot T-Bar was installed and on December 18, 1954 a 6,200-foot Roebling double chairlift to the top of Spruce Peak was dedicated. Then in 1963 a second Riblet chairlift was run alongside the Little Spruce T-Bar but nearly twice as far up the Spruce slopes.

While the Spruce area represented a major expansion it had special significance in another way: with the exception of the small Toll House slopes it was the first lift and trails complex on private property. Nearly two-thirds of the Mansfield ski complex lies within the Mt. Mansfield State Forest, which is to say, on public property.

For the privilege of operating on this land the early Mt. Mansfield lift interests entered into leases with the Vermont Forestry Service (later the Forests and Parks Department) with the first of these dated November 14, 1939. Payment was to be a nominal $1 a year plus 10 per cent of gross receipts over $40,000. It was not until 1946, however, that the state received anything beyond the single dollar. For that year receipts of the Mt. Mansfield Lift Co. reached $43,878.50 and it paid the state $387.85 as 10 per cent of the difference between that and $40,000. Since then the annual payments have grown steadily (and the lease terms have undergone major revision); for the 1968-69 fiscal year the Mt. Mansfield Co. paid $61,937 and for 1969-1970, $57,100.

And so we draw to the end of our story of the Mt. Mansfield Company — at least up to the present; the last chapter will include a look at its future plans. But before closing this chapter a few other matters relating to the company and Mt. Mansfield skiing generally need to be touched on.

One is the Stowe Area (originally Stowe-Mansfield) Association which serves as a booking agency for accommodations at its member lodges. With its office on Main Street in Stowe village it also serves as an information center for visitors and works closely with the Mt. Mansfield Co. in promotion of the area and sponsorship of various special events.

Another is the Mt. Mansfield Ski patrol, some references to which have already been made. The patrol was organized the winter of 1935-36 by a special committee of the Mt. Mansfield Ski Club headed by Albert W. Gottlieb. Initially it was strictly a volunteer arrangement but in 1941 the club hired its first paid patrolman, Fritz Kramer. After the difficulties of maintaining the patrol during World War II the MMSC came back strong with six paid men in 1946-47. But with the growth of skiing the patrol became more than the club could handle and a short while later the Mt. Mansfield Co. took over this important service to skiers. Today the patrol consists of 26 paid members supplemented weekends and other busy periods with a select group of volunteer patrol "alumni."

The ski patrol's principal role is, of course, care of injured skiers. In addition, as part of their safety routine patrolmen "clear" the trails each day after the lifts have closed to be sure no skier, injured or otherwise, remains on the slopes. Each patrolman has had extensive first aid training and the patrol as a unit is backed up with an elaborate telephone network and caches for toboggans and other supplies. (The first toboggans used were made of corrugated iron, a material favored over wood because porcupines would not eat it!) The patrolmen also act as all-round guides and Good Samaritans for skiers, advising them among other things on the degree of difficulty and condition of trails.

Many if not most of Mansfield's skiers stay for more than one day and hence need overnight accommodations. Today in Stowe there are more than 60 inns, lodges and motels with a combined capacity of some 4,500 persons. Two of these closely associated with Mt. Mansfield itself are the Mt. Mansfield Company's Toll House Motor Inn and the Lodge at Smugglers' Notch.

The original little Toll House building, where summertime Toll Road fees were collected, assumed a winter role as well for skiers beginning in 1935-36. In 1940 an addition was built which provided a snack bar, ski shop and warming area plus guest accommodations. In 1949 further expansion and improvements were made to the structure and in 1964 the present Toll House Motor Inn was built which completely absorbed the older building. (Across the way a combination administration building and base lodge for the Toll House slopes had been built in 1948; this burned in 1968 and the following year the present separate administration and base lodge buildings were constructed.)

The Lodge at Smugglers' Notch began in 1923 when Joseph T. Lance acquired what had been the farm home of George Harris and converted it to a rustic summer resort including a number of tent platforms for campers on the grounds nearby. Over the years various expansions and improvements have been carried out under different owners with the Mt. Mansfield Co. acquiring the property in late 1950. The original tentsites are long gone and today a handsome white-clapboard-with-green-trim building set amid spacious, flower-graced grounds provides luxurious accommodations for upwards of 100 guests.

The place is specially known for its award-winning French cuisine which includes what can only be called a spectacular Sunday buffet supper.

The Mt. Mansfield Company's ski development has been the foundation of significant economic gains for Stowe. A miniscule portion of this income to the area is left unintentionally by visitors — the coins and even bills which they drop while riding the lifts or which slip out of unzippered pockets when falls are taken. With the arrival of spring enterprising individuals comb the trails and lift-lines hunting for this money. One such "treasure-hunter" has been Erwin "Lindy" Lindner, who for some years was custodian at the Smuggler's Notch state campground. Returns vary, Lindner told the writer: "A couple of times I've come home with enough to finance a spring fishing trip to Canada but once after a full day's outing all I found was 89 cents." Coin of the realm is not the only thing which skiers lose. Lindner has a rope about five feet long completely strung with keys which he had found — about 800 of them. Two other items he's picked up are more unusual — one was an upper bridge of false teeth, the other a glass eye.

And on that odd note we bring this chapter to an end. Up to this point attention has focussed almost exclusively on the Stowe side of Mt. Mansfield. So like the bear which climbed the mountain we shall now take a look at Mansfield's other side.

CHAPTER
11

The Other Side Of The Mountain

FOR MOST OUT-OF-STATERS and for many Vermonters as well, Mt. Mansfield is Stowe and vice versa. The fact is, of course, that this town includes only the east side of our mountain while the town of Cambridge includes the north end along with all of Smuggler's Notch and the west side lies in the town of Underhill, which also claims the Chin, Mansfield's highest point.

Both of the latter towns very much share in the story of our mountain. For many the view of Mt. Mansfield from the west as it rises steeply from the floor of Pleasant Valley is much more dramatic than the easterly view. As for developments on the mountain, Underhill early on was as active as Stowe when it came to summer tourist trade and later was the scene of two ski areas, one of which remains. Cambridge, with the Madonna Ski Area on the Sterling Range, has something which now approaches Stowe's ski development on Mansfield's east side.

In any event, with Smuggler's Notch in Cambridge, the summit of Mansfield in Underhill and the rest of the mountain's ridgeline in Stowe, public confusion over which town to identify the mountain with is understandable. As will be recalled from Chapter 3, Stowe and Underhill are divided by a zig-zag boundary which runs along the Mansfield ridgeline. The story of that line is a little zig-zagged itself but if nothing else it has led to two hand-me-down stories of "a great landgrab" and jurisdictional dispute between Stowe and Underhill. Both stories relate to the time the original town of Mansfield was divided between the two towns by that zig-zag affair. And both involve the question of which town Mt. Mansfield's Summit House lay in.

One tale was set down some years ago by Emily Flynn, a long-time Underhill schoolteacher. This has it that as a result of the confusion over town jurisdiction, management of the Summit House varied alternate years between Stowe and Underhill parties. "This condition," Miss Flynn wrote, "existed there until much trouble was caused by hilarious young men getting hard liquor at the hotel and neither town having the jurisdiction to stop the sale of it or punish the offenders." To resolve the conflict, her story concludes, Stowe simply sent surveyors to check the town line and ended up with the Summit House definitely in that town.

By another account, Underhill was claiming the whole top of the mountain along with the Summit House. Stowe residents, it seems, wined and dined Vermont's governor and other officials, pointing out to them that since access to the mountain hotel was from Stowe then the Summit House properly should lie in that town as well. These same Stowe citizens then went to work on the Legislature when it next met and lined up enough votes in their favor to capture the Nose and Summit House.

Both tales are based on a thread of reality but from this is woven a fabric which appears to have little basis in fact. What definitely is true is that there has been great uncertainty about the location of the Stowe-Underhill line with the Legislature directing a resurvey carried out in 1862 and the Lamoille County Court ruling in the early 1900's on a dispute over the location of the resurveyed line. But that the Legislature somehow altered the original town boundary or that Stowe by itself did so are both out of the question. On the other hand, the writer cannot say for certain what *did* happen though some evidence was found which suggests a shift — on paper at least — of a portion of Underhill along Mansfield's ridgeline to Stowe. The subject could be an intriguing pursuit for some other researcher.

To Underhill goes the credit for providing the first gateway to Mt. Mansfield and the first facilities on the mountain for summer visitors. That "gateway" was a road from Underhill Center part way up the mountain, a survey of which was ordered in 1830. Just when the road was built is not certain but in 1850 a small hotel was constructed at the end of the road. This became known as the Halfway House, a name still associated with the building's site and a trail up the mountain.

As will be noted in Chapter 12, some sort of trail up the west side of Mansfield had been established by 1847. In 1856 this seems to have been definitely cleared and marked. The Halfway House Trail, as it quickly became known (and still is), was for more than hikers, however. That same year two Underhill men, David N. Shaw and George Downing, provided the first overnight lodging on the summit in the form of a platform tent near the site where the Summit House subsequently was located. Boards for the structure were carried up the Underhill trail by a man and a boy for 25 cents each. Making one trip a day, the man carried four boards at one time and the boy two.

By 1860 and possibly earlier the trail had been improved to become a bridle path all the way to the top of the Nose. That same year or thereabouts a larger Halfway House was built. This was operated by Andre Lavigne and "was well patronized." About 1876 Fred E. Terrill and Charles H. Prouty took over its management and the following year the place is said to have burned. But the writer has come across brief news items in 1881 and 1889 which refer to the Halfway House first as simply "unoccupied" and then as "tumbled down." Thus if there were a fire it would seem that the first rather than the second Halfway House burned.

In 1924 Dr. W.G.E. Flanders acquired the Halfway House property (along with what eventually amounted to about 1,000 acres of land in the area) and put up a new hotel. With considerable publicity about his undertaking he re-established the Underhill side of Mt. Mansfield as a vacation spot of some note. By that year, the state had established the Mt. Mansfield State Forest with a major portion of this running down the west side of the mountain to, and eventually including, the Halfway House site. A major boost for Dr. Flander's enterprise came when the state and town on a joint basis made major improvements to the road leading to the hotel. This project was "completed" in early 1927 though some work seems to have continued after that.

Prior to this time and continuing for several more years, Dr. Flanders was enlarging and improving his premises. At one point he had, in addition to the hotel itself, three large Army tents with cots and blankets which could accommodate 24 camper-guests. He also cut several new hiking trails in the area and relocated a portion of another to higher and drier ground. He also added several features to the hotel itself which are of some interest. One was a telescope on a special tower for viewing the heavens. Another was a sprinkler system to shower the roofs of the porch and dining rooms on very hot days. He also had a searchlight on the upper part of the building. The big light probably helped guests to make their way around the grounds but it also seems to have served as an advertising beacon for the good doctor's establishment.

In the early 1930's, however, personal difficulties apparently overtook Dr. Flanders. He departed the area and the Halfway House was again left to the elements and porcupines. But new life for this high mountain site, if not the hotel itself, was not far off. And as had been the case with Stowe, skiing was the stimulus for a new spurt of activity in Underhill.

While what is now the Underhill Ski Bowl eventually became the principal site of ski development in the town, much of the early activity was on Mt. Mansfield itself. In 1937 some $50,000 in public funds was spent paying federal CCC and state labor to clear a number of ski trails and to build a large parking lot in the Halfway House area. One of these trails — designed by Charles D. Lord, Stowe's master trail engineer, and described as the area's "piece de resistance" — was the Tear Drop Trail. This dropped down from Mansfield's Nose and ran some three miles before connecting with the Halfway House Trail (the Tear Drop is still occasionally used by skiers and now leads further down the mountain). Between this junction and the new parking lot there seems to have been a wider trail, providing something approaching open-slope skiing. A 30-meter ski jump (one account has it as 40 meters) was constructed on a slope just west of the hotel.

Ski activity meanwhile was also occurring on the Eagan Farm just east of Underhill Center. No tows were ever built at the Halfway House area but in 1937 a 1,000-foot rope tow was constructed on a site at this farm which had been scouted out by another of Stowe's emerging ski development principals, Sepp Ruschp. In addition there was a warming shelter and later the slopes were lighted for night skiing. In the late 1930's and during the 1940-41 season these combined mountain and valley facilities were the site for several ski meets sponsored by the University of Vermont Outing Club, including at least two major inter-collegiate affairs.

At this early stage the Underhill development was comparable to Stowe's — and perhaps even better as many skiers preferred the open slopes which Underhill was offering. And its sponsors — initially the Underhill Winter Sports Club and later the Underhill-Jericho Ski Club — had visions of ski trains from New York and Boston giving their area the same boost that Stowe was getting. But it was not to be. With World War II the operation was abandoned.

Following the war the Halfway House area on state land remained quiescent. In 1946, however, John and William Durbrow purchased the Eagan Farm area to revive skiing there and from that has grown today's Underhill Ski Bowl. A few years later William Durbrow bought out his cousin and has operated the area ever since. Facilities now include a disc lift and rope tow with operation on weekends and holidays only; night skiing on lighted slopes is available to private groups. The area's patronage is almost exclusively in-state, drawing from the greater Burlington area and some Franklin County towns.

Credit for the first ski tow in the Mansfield area rests not with individuals in either Stowe or Underhill but to a Jeffersonville man, Wesley Pope. In preparation for the 1935-36 season Pope built his own 1,000-foot rope tow using a 1927 Cadillac engine for the motive power. His description for the writer continues: "It was a baled-hay wire job which I dreamed up out of my own head. It was set up on a south-facing hillside on the Glenn Skiff Farm on Rt. 15 between Jeffersonville and Cambridge village. The location was a big mistake, at least for that winter. It was a slope where there wasn't any snow and I didn't take in a nickel. The following spring I rolled the rope up on a big reel and stored everything away."

But all was not lost for Pope. That summer Craig Burt Sr. contacted him and subsequently purchased the tow for $900 for the developing Stowe ski area on Mt. Mansfield. It was thus a second-hand tow, in installation if not in use, that became Stowe's first.

Jeffersonville is in the town of Cambridge and when you speak of Cambridge you should immediately think of Smuggler's Notch, in which town this mountain pass is definitely located. But unhooking the Notch from Stowe in the public mind has been a continuing problem for Cambridgeites.

As recently as 1968 the Cambridge Community Club launched an effort to get the Forests and Parks Department to permit the erection of a large sign near the town line which would announce to all and sundry coming from Stowe that they were entering Cambridge well before they had reached the Notch. But the department turned down the request out of concern that it would represent an element of the commercialization which it had so carefully removed from this scenic area (a small, standard town-line marker already stood along the road). The club got out some publicity and picked up several hundred names on a petition. Finally Gov. Deane C. Davis responded to a direct appeal to his office by issuing an executive order for the requested sign's erection; this subsequently appeared about mid-1970. The Cambridge Club had had its own sign ready to go but Forests and Parks put up one of their own design. Of this, Mrs. Blanche Gould, a community club member and leader of the effort, told the writer, "Well, it's not just what we planned but it's very nice."

But while a battle was won the war still remains; the Lamoille County Development Council in a special publication of February 25, 1971 about its ongoing comprehensive planning program included a listing of scenic areas in the county which identified Smuggler's Notch as in Stowe.

As for Mt. Mansfield proper, Cambridge and Underhill early on had visions of developments approaching those taking place in Stowe. In 1865 news reached the local press of an idea for a cable-car to be drawn up a track on the west side of Mansfield to the top of the Chin. Nothing further was heard of this but the engineer of the idea, D.C. Linsley of Burlington, *was* heard from again the following year. This time he had a proposal for a toll road up the Cambridge-Underhill side of the mountain. A sponsoring committee was formed to which Linsley subsequently submitted a detailed report on his survey of what he found to be a feasible route. The road was to run from Pleasant Valley to an area not far from the Chin. A "very desirable" location for a mountain house was found near the tiny body of water now known as Bear Pond but which Engineer Linsley christened Eagle Lake at the time. Two charters were obtained from the Legislature for the enterprise and stock sales initiated on both occasions but the new Mansfield road came to a dead end.

Mention has already been made of the road built to the Halfway House. Another road on the west side of the mountain is also of interest though it was principally for logs, not people. This is the so-called Old Traverse Road built in the early 1900's by a lumberman named Harmon Howard. The road ran from an area on Mansfield known as Waugh Basin north around some ledges on Ellsworth Ridge and then south and west to Underhill Center; here Howard picked up established roads for the rest of the trip to his mill in Jericho just across the Underhill town line. For some years logs were hauled in wintertime over the Traverse Road until timber harvesting gave out in the area it was built to serve. The road can still be traced and portions of it are used by snowmobilers and cross-country skiers.

A landmark area at the southern extremity of the Mansfield massif — and the road connected with *that* — provide the final focal point of this somewhat helter-skelter look at the "other side" of our mountain. This is Nebraska Notch. The Notch itself lies in Underhill but the name is directly associated with the Nebraska Valley in Stowe on the other side of the ridge. Local historians have been unable to cite a source for the name but the presumption of this writer is that Stowe residents sometime in the 1800's attached the name of the midwestern state to this valley as a way of signifying its remoteness and largely unsettled character.

Nebraska Notch, while certainly not as dramatic as Smuggler's Notch to the north, has its own share of interesting features and history. Running down the west side into Underhill is Clay Brook along which are various cuts and cascades, two of them known as the 50-Foot-Falls and 100-Foot-Falls. Approaching the Notch one passes between Round Top Mountain on the north and Sugarloaf up close to the Notch itself. Here amid the pile of boulders at the base of some lofty cliffs are the "Ice Cellars," a maze of openings and caves, some of them quite large in which ice can be found the year round.

Also in the Notch area is Peter's Dump, a precipitous incline between the road which once ran through the Notch and the brook below. Tradition has it that in the early days when the road existed Peter O'Jock had taken his horse through the Notch from Stowe to Underhill Center to get some corn ground and incidentally to procure some rum. On the return trip, the rum, it seems, reached home in O'Jock's stomach before the rest of the man reached home himself and at this particular spot he and his horse pitched off the road and down the 60 or 70 feet to the brook. The horse was killed but no one seems to know what happened to Peter except that his name became attached to the place as a result of his mishap.

This book wouldn't be complete without some mention of Indian Joe, the red man who befriended and helped many of Vermont's early settlers in different parts of the state. Two places he is known to have lived are Hyde Park and Morristown just to the north of Stowe.

The story goes that when Joe's father died he was buried in Nebraska Notch. Periodically Joe and his wife Molly would pass through the area, camping near what was to become Moscow village. At these times Joe would disappear for a day or two and was seen going to the Notch, presumably to pay his respects with appropriate ceremonies at his father's grave.

Joe was a member of the Mic Mac tribe of the Algonquin family and was born in Nova Scotia in 1739. An incident in his early life which led to his eventual settlement in Vermont was a raid by the British on his home village. In this his parents are said to have been killed leaving him an orphan. It's the last fact which rather spoils the legend of Indian Joe and Nebraska Notch.

There may be an explanation, however, though it is sheer conjecture. In later years action was taken by the Vermont Legislature to provide a pension of sorts for Joe and Molly. After 1792, when Joe would have been 53 years old, references to Molly ceased in the legislative documents and her apparent death remains a mystery. The couple's marital relations were hardly the best and there is one story that Joe himself pushed his wife over a waterfall to her doom. But could it be that Molly died less ignobly and that Joe buried her, rather than his father, in Nebraska Notch? Joe himself died in 1819 and was buried in Newbury. A monument there is inscribed "Erected in Memory of Old Joe, the Friendly Indian Guide." Perhaps Nebraska Notch is where a similar marker should be placed for Molly.

And so to our story of the road through Nebraska Notch, a road that was, was not and then almost was again.

In the early 1800's a road had traversed the Notch over which teams of oxen hauled produce from the Stowe valley to markets in Burlington. But the coming of the railroad through Waterbury ended the usefulness of the road about 1850 and it was subsequently abandoned. It wasn't long, however, before a call came for its reopening but now with tourism the purpose in mind. A correspondent to a Burlington newspaper identified only as "B." suggested in 1863 the reopening of the Nebraska Notch road and the building of a road through Smuggler's Notch (where only a trail existed at this time). B. felt these roads "would add greatly to the attractions to be offered visitors." It was this idea of a scenic circle tour through the two notches which re-appeared in various publications in 1915 and 1916. But nothing came of the idea at that time though not very many years later the state did upgrade for auto travel the Smuggler's Notch carriage road which had been built in the early 1890's.

In the early 1920's, however, the matter came to a head when Underhill Town Representative Edwin W. Henry, a chief promoter of the Nebraska road, pushed for legislation to have the state carry out the project. His bill apparently was approved but nothing seems to have happened until 1926 when, under pressure by the Mt. Mansfield Civic Club of Underhill, the state Highway Department studied the reopening of the road. In the 1927 Legislature Rep. Thomas J. Maguire, successor to Henry who was now a Chittenden County senator, introduced a bill to appropriate $10,000 to survey and construct the Notch road. But forces alien to the cause prevailed; the Committee on Highways and Bridges came out with an adverse report and the measure died. As the story is now told, a group of property owners in the Stevensville section of the town wanted to preserve the isolation of this area of Underhill just below the Notch and they had enough influence to see to the bill's defeat. Henry and the Mt. Mansfield Civic Club continued to talk up the idea but it apparently never reached legislators' desks again.

That's not where the story ended, however. Some of the road in fact was built though not along the route originally intended. What happened was that State Forester Perry H. Merrill put CCC crews assigned to the Mt. Mansfield State Forest to work extending the Halfway House road towards Nebraska Notch. His hope was to eventually push the road through the Notch and connect the northern portion of the state forest with that to the south in the Waterbury area. About a mile of the road was built but then the CCC program was dissolved and the road work terminated, probably forevermore.

And so Nebraska Notch with its ice cellars and legendary grave of Indian Joe's father today remains untraversed except by foot trails. One of these, known as the Nebraska Notch Trail, leads off from near the end of the Stevensville road and connects with the Long Trail where the latter passes just west of the Notch proper. Continuing across the Long Trail one picks up the Clara Bow Trail, an alternate route for the Long Trail leading to Taylor Lodge a short way to the southeast. The Green Mountain Club's *Guide Book of The Long Trail* provides this description of the Clara Bow; "It is not as easy as the main route but much more interesting, going as it does through the bottom of Nebraska Notch, a rugged and picturesque cleft in the mountain range partly filled with immense boulders. In one place the trail passes under a large rock where there is none too much leeway for big packs, and where a vertical drop is negotiated by a ladder...."

That descriptive note will serve both as a closing to our story of Mansfield's "other" Notch and an introduction to a new story about our mountain as a "heaven for hikers."

CHAPTER
12

Hiker's Heaven

Our course [from the Nose to the Chin] was much impeded by the small firs, which growing to a height of only three or four feet, and their bows being closely interwoven, formed an almost impenetrable barrier [resulting in] a very fatiguing march [of about two hours].

WITH THOSE WORDS did Capt. Alden Partridge describe a part of that climb which he made of Mt. Mansfield in 1818. Today one can make that same summit ridge trek of 1 ½ miles in about one-third of Partridge's time over a well-established trail through and not *over* the dwarfed tree growth which gave him so much trouble.

Partridge also had to bushwhack his way up what was then a trail-less mountain. Today there are ten basic approach trails of varying length and difficulty which together with other branch paths make up a total of about 32 miles of trails on Mt. Mansfield. With its open summit ridge for views and a variety of interesting geological features to explore, Mt. Mansfield has long held a special appeal for the hiker. But without this extensive trail system that appeal would undoubtedly be greatly diminished.

Even without trails, however, residents of the Mansfield area were climbing the mountain at an early date for recreation and interest as opposed to Capt. Partridge's utilitarian purpose. But by 1847 and perhaps earlier there was at least a semblance of a path up the Underhill side of the mountain. It was this trail, now known as the Halfway House Trail, which a few years later was used to haul up materials for that first shelter built on Mansfield's summit. And by 1853 a carriage road had been built halfway up the Stowe side of the mountain with a bridle and hiking trail the rest of the way to the base of the Nose.

Another trail on the west side of the mountain was cleared in 1856; this followed the so-called Maple Ridge and takes its name from that. Some years later, though just when is not recorded, the Haselton Trail on Mansfield's east side was cleared and named in honor of its sponsor, Judge Seneca Haselton, who was a frequent guest at the Summit House and a great enthusiast of the mountain (this trail still exists but is no longer maintained). These were the only trails on Mansfield prior to 1910, a year of great moment for all wilderness trampers in Vermont and hikers of Mt. Mansfield in particular.

On March 11 that year one man's idea of a trail along the Green Mountain Range the length of the state took form with the organization of the Green Mountain Club. Some time later that man, James P. Taylor, reminisced on how his idea took root and how, in somewhat wry fashion, Mt. Mansfield played a role in creating his dream. As a newspaper story recounted it, Taylor "told how he himself started tramping, got lost on Mount Mansfield, almost died of thirst, [and] tried to leave markers so that those who came after him would see the lovely views which he saw. . ."

From that beginning the GMC plunged into the mammoth job of cutting the Long Trail from the Massachusetts line to the Canadian border. It was 21 years in the doing but in 1931 the last section was cleared and the 260-mile "Footpath in the Wilderness" was completed. While a few lodges and shelters had been built by this time, more of these became the GMC's next priority. By 1935 there were 55 and today there are 71, or an average of about one every four miles.

More than half of the GMC members (about 2,500 all told in 1971) join one of the sections into which the club is divided; these sections help maintain the Long Trail and its shelters as well as various approach and side trails. The first such section, known initially as the Mount Mansfield Section and later and since as the Burlington Section, was organized in that city in August, 1910. The first link of the Long Trail from Camel's Hump to Smuggler's Notch, including Mansfield, was cleared in 1911 with Judge Clarence P. Cowles of Burlington, a long-time GMC stalwart, and Craig O. Burt Sr. of Stowe doing the first work in this area.

In no sense is this chapter intended to be a guide to the Mansfield trail system. For that the reader is strongly urged to obtain a copy of the GMC's *Guide Book of The Long Trail*. This includes important detailed information about trails shown on the special GMC map of the Mansfield region which appears in this book. The guide book also provides general advice on hiking and camping preparations, equipment and supplies, and trail etiquette. But here we will provide some descriptive notes and history of several of the trails and shelters on our mountain as well as some details of various hiking experiences.

Working from north to south, the Long Trail itself leaves Rt. 108 a short ways below the state picnic area on the way to Smuggler's Notch. This leads to Taft Lodge, one of the oldest and largest GMC shelters (the trail is also known by that name). It was built in 1920 by our Stowe lumberman, Willis M. Barnes, with funds provided by still another judge, Elihu B. Taft. It's a sturdy log cabin located not far below the Chin with cables anchoring the roof against the sometimes howling summit winds. Beginning the first year after its construction, a caretaker was stationed at the lodge to provide water and firewood, keep it picked up and generally oversee the place. Provision of the caretaker was ended about 1930 but with the growth of hiking interest in recent years the GMC in 1969 again placed a man in charge of Taft Lodge.

Leaving Taft Lodge on the Long Trail one climbs steadily through Eagle Pass and then on up the Chin, the absolute top of Vermont. The next mile and a half to the Nose is along generally open ridge. Before long one reaches the Lower Lip and a little farther the Upper Lip. A trail to the left at the Lower Lip leads to the Cave of the Winds, while a trail to the right takes one to a connecting series of side trails — The Subway, Canyon North Extension, Canyon North Trail and the Canyon Trail. Each of these leads through a variety of interesting and dramatic crevices, chambers, caves and canyons, many requiring some agile manuevering and some with ladders and cables to assist hikers over difficult places. These and several other trails on the summit were originally opened and are maintained by the Outing Club at the University of Vermont.

But continuing on the Long Trail south, one reaches the Summit House site, now the location of the WVNY-TV building, and picks up a continuation of the Toll Road along the west side of the Nose which leads to the WCAX-TV transmitter facilities building. One can branch off in this area for a gradual ascent of the Nose.

The Long Trail leaves the road before reaching the WCAX building and continues on over the Forehead and then down an open ridge and again into the timber before passing through a dramatic opening under large rocks jammed between opposing walls known as the Needle's Eye. Just below this on a side trail to the right is the Mabel Taylor Butler Lodge at 2,920 feet of altitude. It was built in 1933 in memory of a devoted GMC member from Burlington.

From here the main trail continues downhill west of Mt. Dewey and on to Nebraska Notch and Taylor Lodge, named in honor of the GMC founder. First built in 1926 it burned the winter of 1950-51 and was rebuilt the following summer. In 1971 the GMC began providing caretakers at both this and Butler Lodges as well as Taft Lodge.

An alternate approach trail on the west side of the mountain is the Laura Cowles Memorial Trail, named in honor of Judge Cowles' wife. It was laid out in 1931 by the couple's son, John, and was for some years known as Cowles Cut-Off Trail. That in turn was altered by some to Cowles Keep-Off Trail, a kidding reference to its unimproved condition. But work by members of the Cowles family, including the judge himself, and others finally put it in good shape in 1960. In its lower part it passes a number of brooks and springs and then through a charming fernery. Its upper reach is a challenge for more experienced hikers as it approaches the summit ridge.

At the north end of Mansfield, two of the steepest trails in the Green Mountains, the Bear Pond and Hell's Brook Trails, provide approaches from Smuggler's Notch to the summit. The latter follows the course of a small brook from the Lake of the Clouds. Both offer striking views across the Notch and to the Sterling Range.

Back at Butler Lodge is the start of the Wampahoofus Trail, certainly the most colorfully named on Mansfield. This scenic and rugged trail leads up and over rocks and through caves and crevices to a point where 25 or 30 feet above him a hiker spots a large rock in the profile of a grisly and ferocious-looking animal.

It was back in 1933 or 1934 that Professor Roy O. Buchanan of Burlington laid out the new trail (Buchanan is another GMC stalwart, supervising the Long Trail Patrol in its trail maintenance work and directing construction of 23 shelters). He was at the lodge when three boys who accompanied him came back with a report on the peculiar rock. Buchanan went to investigate. As he later told the writer, "I had heard tales of the Sidehill Wampahoofus and when I saw the profile I said, 'There's an ideal Wampahoofus petrified in rock.' And that's how the trail name came to be."

The "tales" Buchanan had heard together form some colorful folklore about an unusual animal which at one time proliferated in Vermont (and may still exist, of course). As a special adaptive feature its legs on one side are longer than those on the other which permits it to navigate with ease the state's mountainous terrain. One account has the Wampahoofus as a small, placid, vegetarian creature something like a porcupine; its canted physique permits easy grazing on round grassy hills. Another account, which gives the name Hill Dog or Side-Hill Winder, describes the animal as a special breed of wild dog able to pursue its quarry around the sloping sides of a hill but not up and down it. This account tells of the animal's fate:

Through long interbreeding within the packs, it eventually came about that all the females were born left-hand, all the males, right-hand runners. Thus, as the males were unable to overtake the females in breeding season, no more winders were born, and an interesting animal has practically disappeared from the earth.

A Sidehill Wampahoofus may yet be found but if not, this illustrious creature at least has a permanent memorial on Mt. Mansfield.

Hiking on Mansfield's trails, as well as the whole Long Trail system, is primarily a warm weather activity. But hardier souls have also done it on snowshoes in the wintertime, particularly before skiing came to dominate the mountain.

One jolly but frigid trip was made in February, 1877 by a party of twelve from the University of Vermont up the west side of the mountain. After lunch at the Summit House they repaired to the Nose to "smoke and talk over the tramp." It was a very short stay, however, for they "reported the velocity of the wind [at] *five hundred miles per hour* and the thermometer *thirty degrees* below zero." The return trip was a lively one: "The game of 'follow the leader' was pretty freely indulged in. Each person seemed to be trying to play 'leap-frog' with himself. At one time there were nine persons in one heap, out of which the snow-shoes were taken by pairs and the owners thus identified."

Another February, this one in 1918, saw three men make a trip from Underhill, picking up the Long Trail and passing through the Needle's Eye. Just above that they stopped for lunch, the menu for which was the most notable characteristic of this trip. The ingredients were, in the order listed: melted snow water, sandwiches of wheat and graham bread, crackers, Triscuit, Shredded Wheat, bacon, boiled eggs, malted milk tablets, cheese, concoction of chocolate, cracker crumbs, buttermilk and raisins, hot chocolate, condensed milk, oranges, and sugared eggs. Oh yes, this was topped off with "Ess-tee-dee Dandruff Cure and Cigars." The threesome continued on to the Summit House and then down the Toll Road, traversing a hazardous ice-coated area and completing the trip by moonlight.

Note of winter outings in the Mansfield area cannot be left without mention of the extra hardy outdoorsman who on November 10, 1935, after a night at Barnes Camp, had himself a swim in Sterling Pond while his wife shivered on shore at a temperature of 41 degrees.

But summer and fall is really the hiking season for Mansfield as elsewhere. Ideally the day for a climb is sunny and brisk and black flies and other bugs are out of season. The upward trek still loses the breath and raises a sweat but that first view through 60 miles or more of clear air brings the accomplishment immediate returns.

Conditions are not always ideal, of course. But the healthful punishment can still bring its own reward. As one party described their trip up cloud-shrouded Mansfield: "All the while we climbed, a gale blew from the west, and condensation from the fog matted our hair and soaked our clothing. The sensation was one of excitement and exhilaration, and every few seconds one of us would pause to exclaim, 'Boy! Isn't this the most?' "

As with any endeavor there's a wrong way and a right way to hiking. The *Long Trail Guidebook* advises among other things the use of "substantial shoes" and sturdy wool sox. Street shoes give out in the rain and those with leather soles are downright hazardous to use on rocky and uneven trails. But there are always a few of the uninitiated who trek over Mansfield ill-fitted to enjoy their hiking in safety and comfort.

This is not a new story, however. A hundred years ago the problem for women trampers was particularly acute as dresses were *de rigeur* even for such vigorous outdoor activity. This is by way of introduction to the account provided by one of a group of young men and women who made a trip from the Summit House to the Chin one day in the early 1860's:

> As a small party set out on this expedition, we earnestly entreated our fair friends to leave their hoops behind, but without avail. Their gallant attendants found constant employment in unhitching them from the brambles and crags, till our return, when passing the lips, a wild gust of wind swept up the mountain side,

followed by a terrific scream from some of the ladies which suggested to me that some of them must have blown over the precipice nearby. On glancing around I discovered truly a fearful state of affairs. The hoops had refused to obey the usual laws of gravity, and were towering upward like balloons: near by was a newly married pair, the blushing bridegroom [tugging] lustily at the canvas to spare the mortification of the unfortunate bride. . . . A general collapse was soon effected and our ladies returned to the summit house wiser if not better women.

Brief accounts of two warm-weather Mansfield hikes of the 1880's introduce a footnote of an entirely different sort to the mountain's history. One of these tells of five young women who in September, 1885 climbed the mountain to spend the night at the Summit House. The next morning they "paid a visit to the mountain hermit, who lives in an extremely airy cabin among the rocks and devotes his time to scientific research." And in July, 1886 a party of young people was on the mountain and explored "a small cave . . . just above the hermit's cottage." From these it appears Mt. Mansfield can claim to have had an honest-to-goodness mountain hermit though the writer has been unable to learn anything else of this mysterious character.

What was claimed at the time as a record *descent* of the mountain — on foot, that is, not on skis — was made by two Stowe men in early August, 1933. After climbing the mountain (how much time *that* took is not recorded), Johnny Harvey, also known as the Stowe Lumber Jack, clumped down the Toll Road from the Summit House to the Toll House in 20 minutes while his companion, Wilfred Salvas, made the same trip in 25 minutes.

And what may have been a record combined ascent *and* descent took place on August 11, 1969 when members of the U.S. Olympic Cross-Country Ski Squad hustled over Mansfield. The hurried visit was part of the team's fast walk and jog of the 260-mile Long Trail as a combination conditioner and fund-raising publicity stunt. Exact point-to-point time records were not kept but the group's leader, John Caldwell of Putney, told the writer they had cut one-third to one-half from the normal hiking time listed by the Green Mountain Club in its *Long Trail Guidebook*.

Another notable climb of our mountain came on August 25, 1970 when professional mountain climber Mitch Michaud of Oregon attained its summit. What gave the ascent special significance was that Michaud was in the process of successfully climbing in the one year of 1970 the highest point in each of the 50 states.

Hikers can and have gotten into trouble on Mt. Mansfield, and we don't mean just with ballooning hoopskirts. The writer found no record of falls on Mansfield itself which resulted in serious injury or death but such accidents have probably occurred and several have definitely taken place in the Bingham Falls area.

People also get lost and that can be a trying experience in itself. An unhappy event of this sort, which has an almost amusing conclusion, occurred about 1849 for a party of young men and women climbing the mountain from the Underhill side. They lost their way, got soaked in a rainstorm but then picked up a brook and followed it downhill to what they hoped would be civilization. A news account completes the story: "Traveling in the water the most of the way, over boulders, through thickets, until more dead than alive, and almost stripped of clothing, they found themselves at a farmhouse in Stowe, at midnight hour. Unwilling to be seen by daylight, they procured a team to Underhill through Winooski Valley before sunrise."

But even with today's complex of trails on the mountain, it's possible to leave one of them for a bit of off-track exploration and then be unable to relocate the trail. For lack of use and lack of maintenance some of Mansfield's trails at different times have filled in with blow-downs and new growth and become hard to follow. And there are walkers who simply wander off the road at the base of the mountain, get disoriented and find themselves in trouble. On a number of such occasions summer hikers lost on Mansfield have been led to safety by local rescuers.

Smuggler's Notch offers special opportunities for difficulties. The inexperienced climber may confidently scramble up a combination of steep pitches, then look down and realize how much more difficult and dangerous it is to return. He (or she) is suddenly trapped.

For Betty Trombley of Winooski and a companion this syndrome of events occurred on a clear and beautiful day in August, 1969. They had climbed well up the Mansfield side of the Notch when they suddenly found they could neither go higher nor retrace their steps down. Their calls aroused other sightseers below and soon help was on the way in the form of Adi Yoerg of Stowe. Yoerg is an expert and highly-recognized Alpine mountain climber who came to the United States from his native Germany in 1953 and joined the Mt. Mansfield Co. shortly thereafter as ski instructor in the wintertime and tennis instructor in the summertime.

By the time he arrived at the scene about 4 p.m. Miss Trombley's companion had been able to work her way to safety. First scrambling to the base of the rock face on which the one girl was still stranded, Yoerg after two false starts reached her in a half-hour of free climbing. Driving a piton he belayed himself to the ledge and tied a rope harness around the girl. He then had to talk to her about five minutes before she felt sufficient confidence to let herself be lowered. It was a full rope-length, or about 120 feet, before she reached a safe point to be released. This successful rescue by Yoerg was his fourth in the area.

Mt. Mansfield is hardly a Swiss Alp but there are a few areas on the mountain where Alpinists have applied their rigorous rock-climbing techniques with ropes, pitons and other specialized paraphernalia. One interesting climb, according to Yoerg, is a rock face near the Cave of the Winds. Another site is the steep north face of the Nose. Yoerg reports of this, however, that "it is wet and mossy and makes for messy climbing. I don't recommend it for pleasure." It is the Notch cliffs that offer a number of challenges to Alpinists and the ascent of one of these provides a special note for this record of mountain-climbing in the Mansfield area.

A diary kept by Robert Bourdon of Stowe carries the following brief entry for October 8, 1963: "Climbed Elephant Head with Adi in Notch. Took a good five hours. First ascent." Adi was, of course, Adi Yoerg, and Bourdon's 14 words is a modest summary of a notable rock climb made by the two men.

The Elephant's Head measures about 400 feet from the base of its trunk to the top of the head, which is the top of the cliff. For expert mountaineers this is quite a short climb but by the Alpine rating system it ranks on a par with the most difficult. This system is based on a scale of increasing difficulty from 1 to 6 with plus and minus subdivisions for the 5 and 6 ranks. According to Yoerg, Elephant's Head can be rated 5-plus and 6 for much of its length with one point a 6-plus. That last category he has described as "suicidal" when attempted alone.

Elephant's Head for some years had been looked over by Alpinists and one other local party had made several partial climbs for reconnoitering purposes but had yet to make a final assault. For their attempt that October morning, Yoerg and Bourdon were at the bottom about 7 a.m. It had rained the night before which made for poor conditions and a high wind came up which added further difficulties. But off they went with Yoerg in the lead.

The first two-thirds of the way was up a long crack. At the top of this is an overhang which Yoerg was finally able to negotiate with a special sling. On the tiny shelf above this they rested and had lunch, then started out again. "It was horrible," Yoerg later recalled. The rock was wet, algae-covered and slippery and the wind would send the rope sailing away from the cliff. Continuing the difficult climb they eventually reached that 6-plus point. It is a stretch of only some 10 to 15 feet but Yoerg has described it with Teutonic understatement as "more than vertical." It offered no place to hammer in pitons, which require a crack for placement, and the two men did not have a rock drill which is sometimes used for such situations. So Yoerg free-climbed this final major obstacle. "I climbed with courage," he said. "I felt that if a fly had landed on my back it would have tipped me over." But he made it and soon had Bourdon up after him. The two then made a final difficult scramble to the top through the scrubby growth which had worked its way down the cliff face.

The climb had taken that "good five hours" (Yoerg says it was four hours with a half-hour rest) while in a mere 45 minutes the men came down the hiking trail which leads to near the top of Elephant's Head. Thus ended the first ascent of this special cliff. But it has not been the last. On September 12, 1970 two Stowe youths, Lewis Coty and Chris Curtis, made the same hazardous climb.

The record of this notable first provides an appropriate conclusion to our review of Mansfield as a "hiker's heaven" for in the following chapter we shall turn record statistician and provide a list of other famous (and maybe not-so-famous) firsts for the mountain.

CHAPTER 13

Famous Firsts

WHITE MAN'S first sighting of Mt. Mansfield by Explorer Samuel de Champlain, the first climb to its summit probably by Surveyor Ira Allen, and the first descent on skis by Dartmouth Librarian Nathaniel Goodrich — all noted in earlier chapters — are among the more significant first-time-events for this highest of the Green Mountains. There are a number of others, a few of which are indeed milestones and all of them providing additional color to this story of Vermont's capstone.

To continue for a moment with skiing firsts, one odd record is that of the first ascent on skis all the way to the Chin via a *non*-Toll Road route. This proved to be quite an adventure. Dr. Edwin H. Steele of Waterbury and Robert Cate of Montpelier were the participants with the latter later leaving an account of the expedition. Early on February 5, 1927 the two were taken in George Thayer's taxi from Waterbury to the foot of Harlow Hill, beyond which the road was not plowed at this time. "As I remember," Cate wrote, "Thayer insisted that we pay him off before he started back because he figured he would never see us again." As events developed, Thayer's demand could have proved tragically prophetic.

The two men started up the road towards Smuggler's Notch and then, after lunch at Barnes Camp and with a heavy snow falling, they picked up the Long Trail and headed for Taft Lodge. With some difficulty they reached the shelter and, after hanging up several blankets to form a sort of inner room around the stove, settled in for a comfortable night.

The next day dawned bright but very cold. Deep and hard-drifted snow made the climb to the Chin relatively easy. It was after reaching this objective that the going got rough. Just below the summit they had entered one of those cloud-caps which often linger on the mountain on otherwise clear days. And at the top, Cate reported, "we were hit by the worst northwest gale I had ever felt. It picked Doc right off his skis and sat him down hard. When I tried to help, it blew me down, too." In the cloud white-out they got their bearings mixed, argued some over that, then noticed that each other's nose was becoming frost-bitten, and finally headed out. "The rocks were mostly ice-covered," Cate continued, "so we took off our skis. Half creeping and half crawling we made our way around the Lips. I was afraid we would be blown over the cliffs if we went along the top or even on the east side, so we kept to the west taking the full force of the wind. . ."

They finally reached sufficient snow to re-harness their skis and happily the cloud-cover cleared moments later to reveal the Summit House only a few hundred yards away. Where it had taken nine hours to come this far, exclusive of stops, they proceeded down the Toll Road and to the bottom of Harlow Hill "without further ceremony" in about 40 minutes.

What has been registered as the mountain's first winter ascent with horses took place the first winter after the completion in 1870 of the Toll Road all the way to the Summit House. Three couples and the daughter of one of them set out first for the Halfway House on a sled drawn by four horses. Here they left the sled and then, with the women on horseback and the men on snowshoes, continued on to the mountain hotel. It was so cold when they arrived that they took the horses inside the building with them. A heavy snowstorm came up that night and the next morning the group found themselves marooned. There was, of course, no communication with the valley at this time but residents there mounted a rescue party. Continues Stowe Historian Walter J. Bigelow of the event: "After hours of shoveling and tramping [the rescuers] opened a path down which the horses could bear the nearly frozen and very hungry women. This experience and narrow escape from death quieted the ambition to drive to the mountain in the winter season for many years."

It is trips up Mansfield in warm weather months which have accounted for several other notable firsts. One of special significance was the first carriage to the Summit House following completion of the upper half of the Toll Road. On June 18, 1870 Henry Phillips conveyed the first paying passengers up in a light wagon drawn by two horses. A short distance before the hotel, road-builder Byron Russell and a crew of men were at work filling in a still-remaining rough spot when the party arrived. As Russell later recounted it, "the men lifted the wagon over the boulders and [Phillips] was able to drive the entire [remaining] distance to the house."

Who was the first to drive an automobile to the top appears lost to history and, for that matter, who were the second and third as well. But we do have a record of the fourth such trip. On Independence Day, 1908 George B. Milne of Barre, apparently on a bet, drove his 30-horsepower Haynes automobile with three passengers up what was then a very rough road for such travel. An account in the *Barre Daily Times* continues: "One of the passengers refused to take the trip back down the mountain. The name of the party is withheld, although the refusal is not so much to be wondered at considering that there are very steep declivities and sudden turns, a plunge over [which] would send one hurtling seven hundred feet, perhaps a thousand, at a sheer drop. It was quite an undertaking..."

Regular passenger "bus" service up the mountain began on June 11, 1919 when an Oldsmobile truck with a combination passenger and freight body made its first run. This was owned by Summit House Proprietor Walter M. Adams and driven by H.B. Blossom. The truck, apparently stripped of some of its normal body work, carried eight people and six bales of hay for a total pay-load of 2,350 pounds. This trip was still before the Toll Road had been upgraded for auto travel and, according to a contemporary news account, "portions of it were so steep that the passengers were obliged to cling to the truck or lose their equilibrium."

When time-records for motor ascents were first kept is also lost to history but with completion of the Toll Road improvements in the early 1920's daredevil drivers apparently began to see how fast it could be done. What was reported to be a *new* auto climb record of the 4½ miles from the Toll House to the Summit House was made in September, 1927 by Max Leon Powell Jr. of Burlington, accompanied by his father, Max, Sr., the latter a principal in the Mount Mansfield Hotel Company which had carried out the road improvements. The younger Powell pressed his LaSalle convertible coupe up in 11 minutes, 5 seconds to surpass "any previous record by three minutes, 55 seconds."

That record was cut substantially in October, 1930 when well-known auto racer Ab Jenkins of South Bend, Ind. drove a stock Studebaker 8 up in 7 minutes, 32.8 seconds for an average speed of about 36 miles per hour. (The road today has a 15-mph speed limit which will give some indication of the hazards involved in this accomplishment.) Lending authenticity to the record was Vermont Motor Vehicle Commissioner Charles T. Pierce who rode along as timekeeper. A newspaper account of the event described in vivid detail how Jenkins churned around the hairpin curves where "a missed turn meant disaster." To all this, Pierce was said to have actually enjoyed the experience "although he watched no scenery on the trip up." The event was staged by the Studebaker company as one of a series of promotional mountain climbs for its "free-wheeling roadster." Jenkins was reported to believe the Mansfield climb to be more difficult than either Mount Washington or Pike's Peak and our mountain later received prominent mention in one of the Studebaker advertisements about the car's hill-climb accomplishments.

As for other wheeled vehicles, the record of the first motorcycle climb also seems to have been lost but in the miscellaneous department is an account of the first party of *four* to make the ascent in this manner. On June 20, 1920 Leonard Gary of Morrisville drove a Harley-Davidson cycle up the mountain with his wife on the seat behind him and another couple in a sidecar.

Oh yes, there is also the bicycle. The first for this — *if* it is a first — came at a late date, September, 1969, when 16-year-old Bill Shook made the ascent in an hour and a half. According to the *Stowe Reporter*, Shook used only "low gear" and "for aficionados of the sport we are advised that the bike had a 42 tooth front chain wheel and 24 tooth rear sprocket with 27" wheels." This writer will leave it to those aficionados to interpret the significance of that.

At this point we leave Mt. Mansfield itself for the heavens above it and the record of the first airplane flight over the mountain and the first, and probably only, delivery of mail by air to the mountain. To begin with, our mountain had its own post office for some years. This was established at the Summit House for the summer months on August 12, 1901 and officially continued until May 31, 1956 or about two years before the hotel's final closing. The literal air mail delivery occurred on September 19, 1920 when Capt. Henry Elmer Stickney of Bellows Falls as pilot and Cornelius L. McMahon of Stowe as passenger took off in a Curtiss airplane from a new airstrip south of Stowe village. They carried with them a telegram, letter and Sunday newspaper for Summit House principal Max L. Powell.

At about 500 feet of altitude they encountered a strong north wind; that and cloud cover over the mountain made for less than ideal flying conditions. It took Capt. Stickney three attempts to get above Mansfield and on one of those the two men hit a downdraft and dropped a thousand feet in a minute and a half. But they finally made it and flying over the Summit House dropped the telegram and letter in a special pouch. What happened to the newspaper is uncertain but it's not likely the two men in the plane were reading it. For as a Burlington newspaper reported the event, Stickney and McMahon were "not expecting such high winds and cold weather [and thus] were not properly clothed to meet it but notwithstanding the unfavorable conditions and the thrilling thousand feet drop the trip was thoroughly enjoyed."

This particular first for Mt. Mansfield was a rather special event in its own right. The mountain has also been the scene of a variety of other historic and noteworthy happenings but for those we shall turn to a new chapter.

Other Special Events

THE YEAR WAS 1859. The Stowe Universalist Church had all but completed its official duties as host for a state convention of that denomination. But one final event remained, a major religious service on the top of Mt. Mansfield. On August 26 many walked or rode on horseback up the Stowe side of the mountain while hundreds more streamed up from Underhill. Altogether an estimated 1,500 to 2,000 people massed for the service which was held in an area on the east side of the Nose forming something of an amphitheatre. The service included prayers, hymn-singing, the rendition by the Stowe church choir of an anthem, "How Beautiful Upon The Mountains," and a sermon. Altogether, by one account, it was "one grand Congregation, to worship God in the great open temple of Nature." It was also one of a variety of special events which have been associated with Mt. Mansfield over the years.

As part of another religious service held the summer of 1863 — in the midst of this country's Civil War — Mt. Mansfield was the scene of some political exposition as well. A Rev. Dr. Kirk led the service for a small group at the Summit House and, according to a report in a Boston newspaper, he:

> . . . took occasion to affirm . . . his ardent Christian faith in the cause of the country. His fervent declarations on that point will not soon be forgotten. The mountain top is renewedly consecrated to the Union cause. . . . And but a few days since a well-known Boston lady, of musical talent, sung the "Star Spangled Banner" from the topmost peak, waving the stars and stripes in accord.

An annual religious event begun in more recent years and now an established tradition is the Easter Sunrise Service sponsored by the Stowe Community Church. The first of these services, for which the Mt. Mansfield Co. provides free lift rides, was held on Mansfield's summit in 1955 and continued there until 1958 when the site was shifted to the top of Spruce Peak. It remained there until 1961 when, with completion of the double chairlift, the service was moved back to Mt. Mansfield where it has since continued. Several hundred skier-worshipers turned out for each of the early years and the number has now grown to 800 or even a thousand.

Weather, of course, is a factor (at least one service has been held after the ski area closed down for the season). As a report of the 1956 service noted, "Those attending had to take it as a matter of faith that it was a sunrise service." The weather was cloudy, windy and chill and the young members of the Stowe band "were ordered to keep a warm mouthpiece — an icy one would freeze to the lips with flesh-tearing results." The church's Junior Choir wore their surplices and its pastor, the Rev. Douglas Brayton, his cassock — both with ski pants showing beneath.

A related and equally popular event — though for different reasons — is the annual Easter Parade. Started in 1939, the event is held at the base of the Little Spruce slopes. Skiers dressed in humorous and colorful costumes compete for prizes, the top award being a season's pass provided by the Mt. Mansfield Co. for the best and most original costume. Of special note is that members of the Lewis Bell family of Momsey, N.Y. have walked away, or rather skied away, with the top prize for 31 of the event's 32 years. A recently-added feature of the special day's special activities has been an Easter egg hunt on skis for children down Ricky's Run, one of Mansfield's trails.

A bit of Mt. Mansfield, or some of its snow at least, ended up in Puerto Rico in January, 1954. Snow sufficient to make 10,000 snowballs was flown in specially insulated bags to the Caribbean island for use in a children's snowball fight held on the eve of Three Kings Day January 6, a traditional festive occasion which forms part of the Christmas observance in that area.

Two years later Mt. Mansfield was the scene of a nationally televised event marking the kick-off of the 1956 March of Dimes fund-raising campaign to continue the fight against infantile paralysis. A highlight was the dedication of a two-ton monument carved from Vermont marble in the form of a dime. This was unveiled by Miss Sarah Jones of Rutland, then 64, who was said to be the only known survivor of America's first recorded polio epidemic which occurred in Rutland County in 1894. The monument, which stands at the base of the Nose near the WCAX transmitter station and may still be seen there, was dedicated to the memory of the victims of that epidemic. Another feature was a huge ice sculpture at Spruce Peak done by Dartmouth students of Dr. Jonas E. Salk, developer of the Salk polio vaccine. Various celebrities on hand included J. Fred Muggs, the famous chimpanzee of the Dave Garroway television show, who donned skis for the first time to the great amusement of the many spectators.

Smaller spectaculars involving lights on the summit of our mountain have been carried out on at least three occasions though the weather for two of them did not cooperate. On September 14, 1931 the Green Mountain Club celebrated the 21st anniversary of its founding with a large gathering at the Long Trail Lodge in Mendon Pass east of Rutland. A feature of the occasion was the lighting of a series of flares from mountaintop to mountaintop along the Green Mountain range. But the weather to the north was such that little was seen in that area of the display of lights, including that on Mansfield.

The Independence Day celebration of 1934 fared better when fireworks were set off on Mansfield's summit to the delight of spectators in Stowe village and elsewhere in surrounding valleys.

In the fall of 1899 steam-boiler engines and dynamos for operating a big searchlight were set up at the top of the mountain as part of Vermont's homecoming celebration for its famous native son, Admiral George Dewey, who had captured Manilla the year before in the war with Spain. The night of nights, October 11, was, however, cloudy and rainy and the aerial display with the big Mansfield light was a washout.

A number of American notables by their personal visits to Mt. Mansfield have added other footnotes to the mountain's story. The register of the Summit House for July 18, 1875 received the name of Theodore Roosevelt, Jr., a 16-year-old student who later became 26th President of the United States from 1901 to 1909.

No Presidents in office have visited our mountain but several of the nation's First

Ladies have done so. On July 10, 1933 Mrs. Franklin D. Roosevelt spent two days in Stowe and the intervening night at the Summit House. In late October, 1963 Mrs. Lyndon Baines Johnson, wife of the then Vice President, joined 100 ladies for lunch at the Lodge at Smuggler's Notch. She returned as First Lady of the land in June, 1967 for another visit which this time included a chairlift ride up the mountain.

On July 23, 1885 the nation's 18th President, Ulysses S. Grant, died. A few months later the *Chicago Herald* carried this report:

> THE CAIRN ON THE MOUNTAIN — A Grant memorial has been started on Mansfield Mountain, Vermont, without money, without authority, without design, without care, oversight or responsibility on anybody's part, and yet bids fair to become an interesting and important monument. It is already so far advanced as to be a noticeable feature of the local scenery, and will attain imposing proportions long before actual work on any other memorial is begun.

What seems to have been the first monument in the country to the famous Civil War general had been started in August by a party of hikers on the mountain. Their pile of stones was (and still is) located a short ways north of the Summit House site and subsequent visitors were asked to each add another rock when they passed by. A few at least did so but the add-a-stone tradition was short-lived and the cairn, which measures a bare four feet high, never attained the "imposing proportions" anticipated for it. In fact the original purpose of the cairn seems to have passed from public knowledge until its resurrection in these pages. (The add-a-stone tradition should *not* be revived, however; as will be noted in Chapter 15 the simple removal of a rock in this area can be damaging to the summit area's alpine-tundra plant life.)

The monument to President Grant received instead a change of name. The Green Mountain Club's *Guide Book of The Long Trail* identifies it as Frenchman's Pile to mark the site of a man killed by lightning. And a point near this cairn was indeed the scene of such a horrendous fatality. On Sunday, September 4, 1898, Mr. and Mrs. Edward Gomo of Essex Junction and a Mr. and Mrs. Billings of Underhill were on the mountain when about 4 p.m. a severe electric and rainstorm swept over them. A bolt of lightning struck right in their midst, killing Gomo and knocking unconscious his wife and the other couple. Help reached them a short while later and the dead man's body and the three survivors were carried back to the Summit House where the latter were treated and subsequently recovered.

That was one of several deaths which have been recorded on our mountain. On September 21, 1921 William W. Patten, 51, of Boston and some companions had hiked to the top via the Haselton Trail and were returning by the Taft Lodge Trail. Nearing Barnes Camp Patten suddenly collapsed and died almost instantly. On January 23, 1970 David Alan Nass, 19, of Harrison, N.Y. was skiing the Nose Dive and only 300 yards from the parking area apparently went out of control and crashed off the trail, suffering head injuries which led to his death a short while later.

On Thursday evening, October 6, 1966, the tower at the Burlington Airport received a request for landing instructions from three Canadians in a twin-engine Piper Comanche airplane. That was the last that was heard from the plane. It was mid-afternoon the following day when a Civil Air Patrol search plane discovered the Comanche where it had crashed into the west side of Mt. Mansfield a short ways down from opposite the Summit House site. Dead in the tragic event were David Sheffler, Robert Rosen and Mary Pert, all of Montreal.

Death has left its mark on Mansfield in another way. On December 21, 1968 Mrs. Elizabeth Loree died and was cremated. In a receptacle at her home had been the ashes of a sister, Miss Laura Thomas, who had died February 5, 1950. The ashes of the two long-time Stowe residents were subsequently scattered from the top of the mountain by personnel of the Stafford Funeral Home. The ashes of several other persons have likewise been flung to the winds from Mansfield's summit, the most recent of which were those of Hannes Lipponer, a long-time Stowe lodge owner, in the summer of 1971.

Several of the more joyous milestones of human life have also occurred on Mt. Mansfield. The *News and Citizen* of Morrisville on September 4, 1884 carried a brief report on "what may be called a marriage in high life." It was the uniting September 2 on Mansfield's summit of Will Town of Morristown and Ida Lilley of Morrisville.

At "high noon" on June 12, 1928 at the very top of the Chin a wedding ceremony was performed for Malcolm Wallace and Cora Stevens, both of Marlboro, Mass. As the *Morrisville Messenger* wryly commented, "The affair was intended to be kept a profound secret, although how it could be kept a secret when the ceremony took place on the most exposed spot in all Vermont is not very evident." The couple's attire for the occasion was quite colorful; Miss Stevens was dressed in "a riding suit, her coat of tan color, hat green, knickers white, and riding boots red" while Wallace also wore a riding suit and cowboy hat.

And on June 18, 1931, "as the sun was dipping shadows of gold and purple over the landscape," Dr. Joseph A. Wark and Merle Joyce Ladd, both of Barre, were united in marriage near the Summit House in another ceremony in Mansfield's great open spaces. Their choice of wedding site was in part because Mrs. Wark's home as a child was in Stowe Hollow from which there was a full view of Mansfield. "My late husband and I," she told the writer, "were also both very sentimental about the state and the Green Mountains and Mt. Mansfield in particular." The family attachment to the mountain remained, with the couple's children subsequently becoming regular skiers there. And Dr. Wark's gravestone also includes an engraving of Mansfield's profile.

The Octagon, specially decorated with balloons, streamers and flowers, was the setting on April 18, 1970 of a party for the announcement of the engagement of Anna Prince and Joseph Haley. "Roni," a columnist for the *Stowe Reporter*, provided a colorful account of the event in the form of a recipe for "Champagne & Strawberries A La Prince." To those items one adds some good music and good friends and then, wrote Roni:

> . . . give it all some real substance and meaning, the vital ingredient. Pansy Prince and Joe Haley, looking like two delicious pink and white Valentines, announce their engagement, followed by thunderous cheers and tears and an ovation which threatened but didn't crack Mt. Mansfield. With the sun setting in the valley below, at Pansy's suggestion, you find someone you love and ski down surrounded by your Mansfield soul-mates. You are convinced it was the best end-of-season recipe, or anything, ever!

Since Mansfield has witnessed both love and marriage what could be more appropriate than to have it the scene for a birth as well. And just that has happened. On September 1, 1901 the wife of Summit House Proprietor Walter M. Adams gave birth to a daughter at the mountain hotel. The new family member was subsequently christened Dorothy Mansfield Adams with the middle name a direct association with her unusual place of birth.

And so with the record of that very special of special events we bring to a close this account of Mt. Mansfield's past. A new dimension is now in order, the mountain's future, and for our final chapter we shall take a look at what may be a critical juncture for old Mansfield.

CHAPTER
15

Of Man and Mansfield

TWO HUNDRED YEARS AGO Surveyor Ira Allen and his party were probably the first white men to set foot on Mt. Mansfield, then but a remote untracked wilderness. Since that time humankind has left its marks on the mountain — roads, ski trails and lifts, hiking trails and shelters, hotels and television antenna. Some residents of the area for which Mansfield provides a noble scenic backdrop are unhappy with the mountain's changing appearance but the old man himself seems so far to have absorbed the change with equanimity. Now, however, there are those who find people are definitely becoming a problem for the mountain and are taking action to preserve its well-being. This concluding chapter will survey Mt. Mansfield's bill of health and what changes appear in store for it.

In Chapter 4 we reviewed the geologic forces which have shaped and altered the mountain. But the plant life growing in its thin covering of topsoil is what gives it much of its character and this vegetation is a vital factor stabilizing the erosive forces of wind and weather on what is a significant watershed for surrounding lowlands. The flora of Mansfield's lower slopes are like those of most Vermont hills and mountains — mixed hardwood and softwood trees with certain species of the latter predominating in the higher elevations. Associated with these is an understory of shrubs, grasses and flowers also generally found elsewhere.

But move onto Mansfield's summit ridge and you enter a different world. It's a world born in the Ice Age 12,000 years ago. It's a world which has been called a "tiny Arctic outpost" because it carries vegetation like that found 1,000 miles or more to the north. Only a few limited areas like this exist in Vermont and the Mansfield ridgeline is said to possess "the finest development of alpine-tundra in the state."

Among the 40 species of plant life in this area of special interest is the extremely rare *Lapland diapensia*, a low compact shrub which grows in little humps and whose beautiful white blossoms appear at the end of May or early June. For the non-botanist there is poetry alone in some of the other plant names: Greenland sandwort, few-flowered sedge, grass-leaved fleabane and hare's tail cotton-grass; also, bilberry, blueberry, cowberry, crowberry, cranberry and creeping snowberry.

Elsewhere on the summit are several small peat bogs where some of the rarest plants in the state are found. One bog is 40 inches deep and is of particular interest. Because the bog is very acid, matter which has fallen in has not decomposed. The result is an extraordinary fossil record of everything which has grown there since the bog was formed some 3,000 years ago. Analysis of the fossil record so far suggests that Mansfield's climate has steadily shifted from warmer and drier to colder and wetter.

The top-most elevations of the mountain have no trees growing on them. But not far down trees do appear though they are strange-looking creatures — gnarled firs and some spruce, most of which are no more than two inches in diameter and only a few feet tall. They are, however, as much as 85 years old. Their dwarfed and spindly appearance is the result of the duress of the high altitude wind and weather under which they have managed to survive.

Mansfield's 4,000-plus feet of elevation makes a substantial difference in the climate under which the unusual assortment of summit plant life survives. In recent years just 78 degrees was the highest summer temperature recorded at the National Weather Service station maintained by the WCAX-Television transmitter crew. That compares to temperatures in neighboring valleys which are frequently in the 80's and sometimes in the 90's. Winters similarly are more severe. The coldest recent winter month was January, 1970 which had an average high of but 7.5 degrees and an average low of 5.25 degrees below zero for a net mean of barely 1 degree above zero. Average snowfall is about 150 inches a year. The winter of 1968-69 saw an extraordinary total fall of 239 inches. Winter is also the time of wind though statistics on this are scarce. The reason for the lack is a revealing one: the winds themselves have blown down the couple of anenometers which have been established at the WCAX observatory. A spokesman at the transmitter station says, however, that winds have probably gone over 100 miles per hour at times.

Another note on Mansfield's climate is its rainfall. Following normal weather patterns for mountains, the rainfall on the summit is substantially greater than that in nearby valleys. Of special interest about its precipitation, however, is that 15 to 20 per cent of the total results from a phenomenon called "fog precipitation." As clouds sweep over the mountain, the needles and twigs of evergreen trees as well as other vegetation coalesce the tiny particles of water to form droplets which reach the ground like ordinary rainfall. The phenomenon itself had been noted some years ago but only recently have careful studies borne out the significance of this special form of precipitation in adding to ground water supplies in neighboring valleys. Ecologists have added this factor to their arguments on the importance of protecting high elevation watershed areas.

For all the hardihood of the summit's Alpine plant life the environment is an extremely fragile one. Hubert W. Vogelmann, a botanist at the University of Vermont, has described what can happen. To begin with, because of the extreme atmospheric conditions, plant recovery from *any* disturbance is very slow — if it takes place at all. If the tundra mat is broken by the removal of a stone or the building of a campfire the wind may soon scour out the thin topsoil and the wound may never heal. Where a tundra area is compacted, even just by the continual tread of hikers' boots, moss will permanently replace the Arctic grasses which have been damaged. Compared to the substantial effects of these relatively mild disturbances, the damage to plant growth of a caterpillar-tread tractor or any motorized vehicle can be severe — and indeed has been on a number of occasions. As for long-term effects, it might be noted that long sections of the hikers' trails along the summit ridge now cross bare rock; these once were covered with the same vegetation which grows alongside the trails.

In Smuggler's Notch is a different, though equally notable, array of plant life. Rare species for Vermont found here are also Arctic-Alpine varieties but being "lime-loving" plants are different from those on Mansfield's summit. The Notch has also been described as "Vermont's grandest fernery" with a number of varieties growing in profusion here. Altogether the Notch has been called "one of the most extraordinary areas of the state from an ecological point of view."

The last 30 years or so have seen the establishment of ski areas on many of Vermont's mountains. Associated with this growth has been the increasing development of upland terrain for vacation home sites. These and other factors have produced reflection in various quarters over preservation, or at least more careful treatment, of Vermont's natural resources. Mt. Mansfield with its Toll Road, major ski complex, array of radio and television equipment and hiking trail network has been one natural landmark of particular concern. In recent years a number of events have occurred in both the public and private sectors reflecting conversion of this concern into action.

In 1970 the Vermont Legislature enacted some significant environmental legislation sponsored by Gov. Deane C. Davis. Basically this sets up a state Environmental Board and nine district commissions to pass on applications for permits for construction and development of land for commercial, housing or industrial purposes. Effects on soil, water, air and natural features are factors which the law requires be considered in issuing such permits. In recognition of the fragility of high elevation areas a provision of the law specifically requires a permit for *any* development of land above 2,500 feet. Vogelmann told the writer that further study of the part mountains play in recharging ground water supplies indicates that the elevation coming under such protection should be lowered to at least 2,000 feet.

On the local level Stowe now has in effect a so-called "interim zoning ordinance." This provides what amounts to "status quo" land-use controls for a limited period of time pending adoption of a permanent, detailed ordinance. Some six years ago Underhill adopted a full-fledged zoning ordinance.

In 1964 Botanist Vogelmann, in a report on significant natural areas in the state, identified Mansfield's summit ridge and Smuggler's Notch as two such "ecological sites of public importance." In early 1969 some 3,850 acres of the Mt. Mansfield State Forest were officially established as a "natural area" by the Vermont Department of Forests and Parks under a 1967 law providing for such designation. This includes the Smuggler's Notch ecological site but not the Mansfield summit site because the latter lies within that 80-rod strip owned by the University of Vermont.

Though hiking and cross-country ski trails are permissible in this special area no downhill ski trails will be cut and no roads or commercial developments allowed (the designated area excludes the existing Mt. Mansfield and Madonna Mt. ski developments). Logging will be permitted only to recover major storm blowdowns or to log areas of the state land which are contiguous to timber harvests on adjoining private land.

In October, 1969 a private organization of volunteers known as the Green Mountain Profile Committee was formed with Botanist Vogelmann as its chairman. The group has acted on several fronts to counter what it contends is a serious threat to the Green Mountains caused by over-development and mis-use. Among other things it was active in the enactment of the state environmental legislation regarding high-elevation land mentioned above. It continues to work to educate Vermonters as to the fragility of mountain terrain, to promote balanced land use planning and controls for these areas, and to preserve mountain wildlands through acquisition of property itself or easements for its controlled use. In this last area, the Committee in affiliation with The Nature Conservancy, a national conservation organization, played a key role in 1970 in the acquisition by the state of that 1,900-acre addition to the Mt. Mansfield State Forest. This was part of a total purchase of 6,400 acres with the balance a large tract in the Camel's Hump area.

As for the Green Mountain Club, since its inception it has encouraged use of the Long Trail system. But as GMC President Shirley Strong recently reported to the club's membership, "With the increasingly heavy use of the Long Trail it is not necessary or even advisable for the Club to promote its use. The appeal of the mountains and hiking is strong today and its use is assured!"

The club has already taken some steps to handle the growing number of hikers. As noted in Chapter 12, the shelter caretaker program has been re-established; this includes a man at each of the three Mt. Mansfield lodges. In addition to normal caretaking duties, these men serve to educate the hiking public about the fragile environment of high elevations and about the GMC's new policies intended to enhance and protect that environment: no dumping of refuse ("pack it in, pack it out") and the limited use of campfires, particularly where suitable firewood is getting scarce, and the use instead of portable gasoline stoves. On another front the club is working with the Forests and Parks Department on methods to deal with trail erosion problems. New emphasis on environmental concerns is also incorporated in the 1971 edition of the GMC's *Guide Book of The Long Trail* and other club publications.

Mansfield itself is receiving the club's special attention and with reason: a detailed study of the summit tundra area showed what Vogelmann has termed an "alarming" diminution of plant life as a result of the simple compaction of people walking over it. The GMC's Burlington Section in 1971 set up a committee to work out a program for improved use and management of the summit area. Among other steps has been assistance in enforcing a total ban on camping and open campfires in non-designated areas. The committee, with help from the Forests and Parks Department is also conducting a traffic flow study for all uses made of the summit area — hikers, lift riders, Toll Road drivers and workers at the several communications facilities. One area of particular interest is determining the volume of foot traffic on the summit ridge originating from the gondola lift.

The University of Vermont for its part has recently taken a new look at its responsibilities regarding that 400-acre tract conveyed by W.H.H. Bingham and John B. Wheeler back in 1859. A special committee was formed in 1970 to make recommendations regarding management of the property. In a report submitted to UVM President Edward Andrews the committee noted that restrictions of the property deeds require in effect "that use of the area be devoted to educational and scientific purposes." "The University," it continued, "has not been able to abide by the spirit of this commitment." This is an implicit reference to the various communications facilities now on the University property.

The group's initial concern was a request from the Vermont Public Safety Department for expansion of its communications building. The upshot was a University decision to construct a single new building in the Nose area to house this agency's facilities as well as those of a number of other agencies, both public and private, which have sought to place communications equipment on the summit. The intent of the move would be to avoid a further proliferation of little buildings and antenna towers. The resulting removal of the present Public Safety building would help to save from obliteration that special Arctic bog noted above which lies in the building's immediate area. At this writing, however, the new building idea is being held in abeyance until the status of the existing WVNY-TV building is resolved. If that should become available, UVM Executive Vice President Wayne Patterson told the writer, other communications facilities might be consolidated there instead.

The WCAX-TV and Educational Television buildings and antenna would, in any event, remain as separate units, though beyond the single consolidated building the UVM committee saw no need for major additional construction in the summit area in the foreseeable future. Patterson noted that television facilities on Mansfield's summit in fact may "soon" become obsolete. Within 20 years, he said, television signals are likely to be beamed directly from a station's valley studio to a stationary satellite in space for retransmission to viewers on the ground.

The UVM committee also made several recommendations relating directly to hikers. One urged the relocation of a portion of the Long Trail away from the area of particularly fragile growth which it now crosses. GMC President Strong told the writer the club is anxious to cooperate but she believes that altering hikers' established patterns onto a new trail would be difficult, particularly when the existing trail would remain visible for a long time because of the slow recovery of natural growth.

Will these various measures and steps be enough to preserve Mt. Mansfield's well-being? Indications are they will not. Continuing population growth together with increased leisure time means ever-growing pressure on the mountain as one outlet for outdoor recreation. A limitation on human traffic of all kinds on Mansfield may be a step not too far in the future. Nobody has yet come right out and urged this but the possibility has been mentioned at GMC conferences and has appeared in print.

Such a future course may indeed be necessary in the view of Sepp Ruschp, president of the Mt. Mansfield Co. He suggests that concerned state agencies and private organizations should be requesting funds from the Legislature "to provide for an orderly system of traffic flow" on Mansfield as well as other Vermont mountains. Such is the pattern long established in European mountains, he points out. Ruschp's feeling is that the Mansfield summit area is public land which is there for people to enjoy. Its use and development should be in keeping with the environment, yes, but to isolate it in pristine condition for the private enjoyment of a few botanists and protectionists, no. And if that means the loss of some of the summit's plant life, then so be it.

To the claims of some that the gondola lift is substantially increasing foot traffic on the summit, Ruschp maintains that the vast majority of gondola riders do not leave the Cliff House area. They may take a walk on the very short trail provided in the immediate neighborhood but most simply enjoy the view, perhaps have a refreshment and then make the return gondola trip. It is not the average gondola rider, he states, but only a few hikers that litter the mountain's trails, vandalize the shelters and create the real threat, if there is one, to the summit's environment.

The company itself has had to take some direct measures of an environmental protection character. In 1970 it issued a summertime ban on all unauthorized vehicles on company ski trails and work roads including motorcycles, trail bikes and jeeps. Erosion developing from ruts created by such vehicles was a reason for the action. And in early 1971 the Mt. Mansfield Co. and Madonna Corp. together announced a policy prohibiting the operation of snowmobiles at the two neighboring areas. Damage to ski trails, law enforcement difficulties and problems of rescuing distressed snowmobilers were cited as reasons for this ban.

On the positive side, Ruschp points out that the company is helping to provide some supervision of Mansfield's summit area. It is paying part of the salaries of the several Forests and Parks Department wardens now stationed on the mountain (the University of Vermont also pays part of this expense) and provides accommodations for one warden and his family.

As for future growth, the company has an established plan for the 1970's. A key element is the creation of vacation home developments in three areas at the base of the mountain. In this regard Ruschp states that he is a strong supporter of and closely complies with the state's new environmental control laws. "This is a good thing for *good* developers," he says, indicating that those who would otherwise be irresponsible developers are discouraged by the laws from proceeding.

The first of the three developments is an eight-acre site for condominiums adjacent to the Toll House slopes (a local Environmental Board commended the company's plans for this). Other development sites are areas near the Lodge at Smuggler's Notch and in the Spruce Peak area where several private homes have already been built over the last ten years or so. The units constructed will be "of the best quality," in the words of one company official, and "they will be done right" with careful planning, construction and landscaping (the company has long taken pride in the design of its buildings and the liberal use of flowers and other plantings on its well-groomed grounds). The company will follow no rigid timetable for numbers of units to be sold each year; rather the residential developments will proceed at whatever pace the need dictates.

As for additional uphill and downhill ski facilities, one new lift is planned with construction expected in the mid-1970's. The schedule for this lift, which will provide access from the Toll House area to the other Mansfield uphill facilities, is tied to the Toll House and Lodge area residential developments so the time for its construction is keyed to the rate of growth of those developments. The company also plans some additional ski trails in the area between the Lodge and the mountain served by the new lift.

And so we close our story of Mt. Mansfield though it's a story, of course, which still continues. What we have recorded here about this mountain is a good illustration of the paradox which occurs when man moves into the fastnesses of nature: that intrusion can affect, sometimes drastically, the very wilderness in which he now finds so much interest and enjoyment. Mt. Mansfield's future will really be the story of finding a balance between the needs of both man and mountain.

Author's Note

A problem for this author, and I presume for other non-fiction writers, has been that much of the material gathered in my research could not be included in the final manuscript because of space limitations. Information which I have left out was, of course, of lesser importance and consisted generally of various supporting details to the main facts, stories and incidents that are included in the final text here. But a few more substantive items also had to be scratched in my final editing.

All of this omitted information was, however, incorporated in my first draft as well as footnote-references to sources consulted, which were numerous. For any who might wish to delve further into some part of the story of Mt. Mansfield provided here I will be presenting a copy of this first draft to both the Vermont Historical Society and the Stowe Historical Society. In the latter case, some of the original sources (or copies of them) will also be furnished.

I am indebted to both these organizations and in the case of the Stowe Historical Society, to several of its members. for their considerable help. A great many other persons — too many to list individually — also furnished invaluable assistance for which I am deeply appreciative.

Robert L. Hagerman

Morrisville, Vt.
September 2, 1971

Index

(Page numbers in *italics* refer to illustrations)